Mysterious Signs Of The Torah Revealed In LEVITICUS

Dr. Akiva Gamliel Belk

- Founder -

jewishpath.org

B'nai Noach Torah Institute, LLC
http://www.bnti.us

Copyright © 2014

All rights reserved.

ISBN-10: 0615982336

ISBN: 13: 978-0615982335

Publisher

B'nai Noach Torah Institute, LLC

Post Office Box 14

Cedar Hill, Missouri 63016

talk@bnti.us

First Edition 03-02-2014

DEDICATED

When I was down you were there
When I needed a friend to listen and share
You were the one to care

When it was difficult and I felt despair
A voice would say, 'I am aware.'
I am here to heal, help and repair

When darkness burdened you would declare,
With me intensely, Shema Yisroel in prayer.'
For this and more I am thankful you are there.

A wife of accomplishment is rare…
Upon you I heavily rely… you are there
The Love you bestow on me I cannot compare…

So I want to thank you for all you took care,
Thank you dear little flower of blossom alair,
Kah Nah Naw Har Raw, you make us a pair.

Akiva Gamliel

Mysteries Of Ha Torah Revealed In LEVITICUS

Table of Contents

DEDICATED..5
Mysteries Of Ha Torah Revealed......................6
FORWARD...9
PREFACE...13
ACKNOWLEDGEMENTS....................................17
INTRODUCTION..19
Offerings, Sacrifices, Tributes and Tefilliah........25
    Chapter 1..25
Living Separated..81
    Chapter 2..81
Grading Our Holiness 105
    Chapter Three..105
Change the World with ONE Action 119
    Chapter Four..119
Sanctifying An Unclean House At Passover....133
    Chapter Five...133
Guarding Against Sin.......................................147
    Chapter 6..147
Parshat Acharei Mot..147
    Chapter 7..161

Parshat Kedoshim..161
Defining Holiness..187
    Chapter 8...187
Parshat Emor..187
Gematria Tefillin 570.......................................201
    Chapter 9...201
Parshat Behar..201
GEMATRIA CHART...237
SCRIPTURE INDEX..238
GEMATRIA'S..242
About The Author..243
Books By Dr. Akiva Gamliel............................246

FORWARD

We are only scratching the surface when we try to study the book of Leviticus. Vayikra is a very deep book!. My husband, Rabbi Akiva Gamliel has spent a tremendous amount of hours explaining this text in a way that is more accessible to us who have not had the opportunity to study it in depth, in Hebrew. English translations just do not provide the best explanations for the original text. The Gematrias that he shares so well brings so much more meaning to each part of this text that we study.

Until the Creator of the Universe restores our Temple we should do our best to gain an understanding of what the Holy One of Israel Requires so that we will be ready to take on those duties – most of these belong to the Kohanim, but we must all be ready to participate as directed by the Torah.

Leviticus is a book with many directives for the Kohanim, the priests who served in the Temple. It may seem like it's just for them. However that is not the case at all. My husband brings truths to the surface that will amaze the reader.

There are some who say these Priestly duties have been done away with, without any consideration of the prophecies that teach these duties / sacrifices will indeed return once the Jewish Messiah comes and the Third Temple is restored.

So much is misunderstood and misinterpreted about these sacrifices. There is a mystical part of these sacrifices that is almost never seen. What is in the physical world, through the sacrifice, returns to the spiritual world that we cannot see. The spiritual world often operates exactly opposite of the physical world we live in.

The word *Karbanot* is usually translated as sacrifices or offerings; however, both of these terms suggest a loss of something or a giving up of something. The word *Karbanot* comes from the root Qof-Resh-Bet, which means to draw near, and indicates the primary purpose of offerings is to draw us near to God. Until that day, remember...

The sacrifices of God are a broken spirit; O God, You will not despise a broken and crushed heart, Psalm 51.19.

Rebbetzin Brachah Rivkah Belk

PREFACE

There are many struggles for those of us who attempt to put pen to paper. There are always struggles. The struggles can make the author's path one of great challenge. Authors and publishers set these arbitrary deadlines we would like to meet for publishing. I often miss them. I study, write, research, proof, edit, rewrite etc. Sometimes it is necessary to set the book I am writing aside for a week, a month a year or more. I am writing books that are resting and waiting somewhere along the path to be completed and published. Rushing to complete a book does not work well for me. Yet, once the book is written I rush everyone up the ladder to get the book published. Struggles with writing and researching is different from human struggles. There are writers and then their authors. Due to our Creator's Great Kindness and assistance I am a writer and an author of many books.

Writers face struggles that prohibit them from becoming an author. Things happen in a writer's life that cause them to put the pen down and throw up their hands so to speak. Only God in Heaven Knows the amount of time that goes into authoring a book. This book is one of those books that rested more than once along the path to publishing. Looking back I can understand a little of why this particular book in part required several resting periods. The earliest portions of this book were written more than fifteen years ago. My writing style has changed much over the years... My attitudes have also changed... So I feel like this book has benefited from these times of rest. I am greatly thankful to the Creator for the revelations written in this book that He has permitted me to see. Dear Reader, these revelations come at a cost. King David was greatly inspired. Where did his great inspiration come from? We do not know the many Psalms David wrote in the mid of night or at the onset of battle or on the road of escape from enemies... Yet, Thank God David shared The Psalms with us. The suffering and the hurting and the experiencing are all part of the beauty that buds forth like a fragrant red rose.

Dear Reader, there are struggles beyond what an author experiences. These are the struggles of those that I dearly love. They impact me also. Their pain becomes my pain. Their issues become my issues. There frustration becomes my frustration. Yet, let us not forget each of these are in The Creator's Control and at His will.

There are also many many happy wonderful experiences that impact the writing of this book. They are all here, the wonderful and the not so wonderful the happy and the sad.

Dear Reader, in this book I have labored to share a Gematria from each Parshat of Vayikra / Leviticus and much more. The Gematrias open new revelations to us that we can understand. The revelations are not new. They are new to us. There are many authors saying the same things... DIFFERENTLY! It is my hope that the revelations and stories I share will touch the depth of your being. It is my hope and my wife's hope that Mysterious Signs Of The Torah Revealed In LEVITICUS will be an eye opener for you and bring about many Blessings.

ACKNOWLEDGEMENTS

Oh Creator of the Universe, thank You for this opportunity to share the Gematrias Revelations in this book the stories and Ha Torah... Thank You for forgiving us of our every sin. Thank You for helping us to return to Torah Observances. Thank You for daily assisting us with efforts to improve. Thank You for every blessing. Thank you for the bread of life. Thank you for Revi... Kaw Naw Nah Haw Raw.

My wife, Revi is a soft spoken, quite, tiny lady, in physical stature, but very big in showing others love, kindness, patience and Observing Torah Mitzvot. I love you Revi and thank our Creator for every breath He Has Given Us! Kaw Naw Nah Haw Raw. Revi thank you for assisting greatly with the editing and formatting of this book. I greatly appreciate your every effort especially knowing some of life's struggles that we faced with great courage and forbearance during this authorship.

INTRODUCTION

I am not a fan of introductions to books. It is important to read a book and to determine for ones self what each chapter is about. There are so many ways of viewing what is written. I feel like my introduction might miss the important points that the reader may receive and that these points may be quite different than the introduction. Each of us have subjects that are intriguing to us and if we read what the author states the chapter is about we may find it uninteresting. This could lead to missing several real important sentences that the reader may consider invaluable. Through the years this has happened many times for me. So I often do not read the forward, the preface or the introduction until after I read the book. So I offer a few comments about each chapter realizing they are grossly inadequate.

The title in Chapter one tells the story. There are Offerings, Sacrifices, Tributes and Tefillah / Prayer. There is a great deal of misunderstanding outside of Judaism surrounding Offerings,

Sacrifices, Tributes and Tefillah / Prayer. There is a difference between Offerings, Sacrifices, Tributes and Tefillah / Prayer. The differences are distinct even though religions have muddied the waters. I explain what Offerings, Sacrifices, Tributes and Tefillah / Prayer are and how they differ from each other. In chapter one we learn about our Creator's Instruction on repentance, salvation and the life here after. The first chapter is long. This was necessary to explain and establish important points regarding repentance, forgiveness and salvation carried throughout this book.

Chapter two discusses Holiness, i.e. the separation of The People of Israel through The Observances we are required to follow. This is a compelling discussion of the separation of Aharon Ha Kohen Gadol and his sons Ha Kohanim as well as the separation of The People of Israel. The indivisibility of the concept of separation with Judaism is conveyed. The discussion ponders the power of the Tent of Meeting and higher levels of spiritual awareness that we are drawn towards.

In Chapter three we take the discussion of Holiness to a different level. One must examine themselves. We use a story to illustrate this. Finding the right balance is not always so easy. What does one do? How do we approach judging ourselves?

In chapter four we note the power of just one positive action. Then we try to carry this to the next step which is for us to follow this course. We should try doing at least one positive action. We should follow the outcome of our action.

In Chapter five we discuss the path of liberation from issues that have held us down, caused us to sin and have held us back. We learn how to reverse improper behaviors. We learn there is a season / festival of freedom and how this applies to overcoming things hindering us, i.e. humankind

Chapter six is about guarding against sin. We, the Jewish People have an important responsibility of Guarding the Observances of Ha Torah while the world is trying to pressure us to turn away from our Observances. This requires a great deal of understanding with non-observant Jews and religions that teach pseudo doctrines.

Chapter Seven is a call for The People of Israel to live like the light we are supposed to be. The focus is on how we must be different from the rest of the world when it comes to relationships. How should be treat others? The Torah lays this out for us. To a degree the entire book centers around the lessons learned in this chapter and in the final chapter.

Chapter eight begins with the misconception of what it means to be Holy. So we begin developing and considering what Holiness is.

In Chapter nine we discover the Blessings of Observing the Command to wear Tefillin.

Chapter Ten explains a very, very import point to The People of Israel, to The People of Noach and especially to Christians who believe Jesus did away with the Old Testament. We discuss why The Land of Israel is Holy! This is a must chapter. The information is crucial for each of us!

I am saying that if Christians were correct about Jesus doing away with all the Laws recorded in Ha Torah then there would no longer be a Holy Land or a Holy City, Jerusalem or a Holy Temple. All of these would be gone if the 613 Commands of Ha Torah were done away with. I am saying that it is the 613 Commands of Ha Torah that make The People of Israel / The Chosen People, i.e. The HOLY People of Israel and make the Holy Land 'HOLY' and make, the Holy City, Jerusalem 'HOLY' and make The Holy Temple 'HOLY'. Nothing is Holy just because we label it holy. There is a meaning to Holiness that is much deeper than just a label!!

The next few blank pages are there for the reader to take notes. Please take notes. Write down questions.

Offerings, Sacrifices, Tributes and Tefilliah
Chapter 1

Vayikra / Vayikra
Leviticus 1.1 – 5.26

Vayikra 1.1 - 2

וַיִּקְרָא אֶל־מֹשֶׁה וַיְדַבֵּר יְהוָה אֵלָיו מֵאֹהֶל מוֹעֵד לֵאמֹר:
דַּבֵּר אֶל־בְּנֵי יִשְׂרָאֵל וְאָמַרְתָּ אֲלֵהֶם **אָדָם כִּי־יַקְרִיב מִכֶּם קָרְבָּן לַיהוָה** מִן־הַבְּהֵמָה מִן־הַבָּקָר וּמִן־הַצֹּאן תַּקְרִיבוּ אֶת־קָרְבַּנְכֶם:

Leviticus 1.1 - 2

And He Called to Moses, and the Lord Said, to him from the Tent of Witness Saying, Speak to the People of Israel and say to them **if Adam, [a man] among you brings an Offering to the Lord from** animals, from the cattle, and from the sheep you shall bring everything from Aleph to Tav of your offering.

The קָרְבָּן Karbon / Offering is offered at a particular place. How do we know this? '...*if Adam, [a man] among you brings an Offering to the Lord...*' The Offering is brought to The Lord. Where is The Lord? The Lord Spoke to Moshe from the Tent of Witnesses. Any where will not do! In Leviticus the offering is offered at the entrance to the Mishkon / the Tabernacle. This is the place where the Presence of the Lord dwells. This teaches us that there is a place for our offerings. Before offerings were made at the entrance of the Holy Tabernacle offerings were made at the place of our formation. Tributes were originally made at the place where the Lord God Formed Adam and Eve from the dust of the ground. Rabbi Nosson Scherman, The Stone Edition The Chumash Travel Size (Mesorah Publications, Ltd., Brooklyn, N.Y. 2001), p. 39

Animal sacrifices did not begin until after the flood of Noach. For the first 1,648 years prior to the flood animals were not sacrificed. Taking the life of an animal was forbidden! (Genesis 9.2-5) The Tributes / The Gifts of Kayin / Cain and Hevel / Able in Genesis 4.3 - 5 are often translated 'offerings' yet No animal life was taken. The Word many translate for Offering is מִנְחָה Minchah which is a gift or as a tribute. The act of taking an animals life was not done during the first 1,648 years. There were no offerings no sacrifices. There were only tributes and gifts. Kayin / Cain, the older brother of Hevel / Able gave a Tribute of spoiled flax seed. Kayin's Tribute was rejected by the Lord! Kayin's Tribute was NOT from the best of his vegetarian produce. Kayin's Tribute was not from the first fruits of his vegetarian produce. Kayin's offering was NOT rejected because it was vegetarian. It was rejected because of Kayin's stubbornness and stinginess.

Hevel's Tribute was NOT a blood offering!! The Torah portion of the Bible says Hevel's Tribute was from the very best of his firstborn flocks. Our Sages Teach this means Hevel brought the finest spun wool. Hevel brought the finest cream and cheese. Hevel's Tribute was accepted because of the correct attitude in which he gave his Tribute to The Lord.

Bereisheit 4.3

וַיְהִי מִקֵּץ יָמִים וַיָּבֵא קַיִן **מִפְּרִי הָאֲדָמָה** מִנְחָה לַיהוָה :

Genesis 4.3

And it happened in the process of many days that he, Kayin / Cain brought **from the fruit of the ground a Tribute** to The Lord.

Kayin brought his Tribute to the Place of the future Altar of the Bet Ha Mikdosh / The Holy Temple. This was the most Holy Place outside Gan Eden. It is the place where our Creator Took from the dust of the ground to form the body of Ha Adam. Rabbi Nosson Scherman, The Stone Edition The Chumash Travel Size (Mesorah Publications, Ltd., Brooklyn, N.Y. 2001), p. 39

Bereisheit 4.4

וְהֶבֶל הֵבִיא גַם־הוּא **מִבְּכֹרוֹת צֹאנוֹ וּמֵחֶלְבֵהֶן** וַיִּשַׁע יְהוָה אֶל־הֶבֶל וְאֶל־מִנְחָתוֹ :

Genesis 4.4

And Hevel / Able, He brought **from the firstlings / the first born of his sheep and** *from the fat [the choice of] / the cream from the milk and cheese, and He, The Lord Had Regard to Hevel and to His Tribute.*

Bereisheit 4.5

וְאֶל־קַיִן וְאֶל־מִנְחָתוֹ לֹא שָׁעָה וַיִּחַר לְקַיִן מְאֹד וַיִּפְּלוּ פָּנָיו :

Genesis 4.5

And to Kayin's and to his Tribute there was no respect and he, Kayin was angry towards [himself], and His face showed great disappointment.

What is the difference between the Tributes?

1.) Kayin did NOT bring a choice Tribute.

2.) Kayin did NOT bring a Tribute from the first of his crops, i.e. מִבְּכֹרוֹת .

Hevel brought a choice Tribute. The Word וּמֵחֶלְבֵהֶן Voo May Cheh Lih Vay Hehn is deep because of it's meaning. The root Word has several meanings which apply in this Verse. Hevel brought a choice Tribute. Why was Hevel's

Tribute considered a choice Tribute? First is because Hevel gave serious thought to his selection. Hevel's Gift to the Lord was not thrown together. Hevel's gift was contemplated, planned and carefully prepared. There are grades of cream, cheese and wool. Hevel's flocks were separated. Separation is a form of Holiness! The בְּכֹר Bih Cohr, first born of Hevel's cattle were separated from the other cattle. The quality of the produce from the first born cattle were graded and separated. This is a higher step of holiness. Then the highest quality of the produce was carefully prepared by Hevel to present as a Tribute to The Lord. Hevel prepared the finest cream, butter, cheese and wool. This was the highest step of separation / Holiness. It was for these reasons that Hevel's Tribute was honored and selected. It was not a sick mangy runt or from the poorest produce from his flocks. Ha Torah equates a firstborn to the Words Yaakov / Jacob Spoke to Reuvein his first born. Let's examine his words to get a better idea of the Scriptures intent regarding a first born.

Genesis 49.3

Reuvein /Reuben, you are my firstborn, my strength, and my initial vigor, foremost in rank and foremost in power.

Yaakov described why the firstborn is the choice. The first born is the cream of the crop. So in a similar way we can understand that one of the issues with Kayin is he was stingy. He did not want to give the Creator anything of value. He wanted to give the Creator something that he no longer had use for.

Think of Kayin like this. If a friend were to tailor a shirt for you out of left over scraps it maybe a nice shirt but it came from scraps. No matter how nice our scraps maybe and no matter how beautiful we can transform our scraps the fact remains we do not give our scraps to The Lord the Creator of The Universe as Kayin did. Compare the difference. If this taylor went into a fine fabric store and purchased the finest and most costly materials with the intent of using his / her's greatest tailoring skills to design and produce the best possible shirt this would be what Hevel did and what Kayin did NOT do. Now let's put this in perspective a little more. I have heard the stories of many children whose parents took cloth from grain sacks and made them nice clothing. I understand. At that time they could not afford more. This was NOT the situation with Kayin. He could have afforded to give the best crop to the Creator but did not. Kayin could have prepared and planned his Tribute instead of throwing something together for the Creator of the Universe. Kayin was unwilling to give or spend. He was not generous. He was stingy. He was stubborn. He was unwilling to open his hand to the Creator let alone the poor and destitute. If one will not select the best, plan and prepare for the Creator and Judge of the Universe then what will that one do for those who are the least? Kayin's lack of generosity was a sin. Kayin was disrespectful to the Creator. Kayin's gift was garbage. Our Sages Say Kayin offered as his Tribute spoiled flax seed. This was a sin! Can we now understand why Kayin's offering was rejected? Kayin had issues with acknowledging and honoring the Creator. Kayin's thoughts and actions were sinful.

Deuteronomy 15.4-8

But there shall be no poor among you; for the Lord Shall Greatly Bless you in the land which the Lord your God Gives you for an inheritance to possess it; Only if you carefully listen to the voice of the Lord your God, to take care to do all these Commandments which I command you this day. For the Lord your God Blesses you, as He promised you; and you shall lend to many nations, but you shall not borrow; and you shall reign over many nations, but they shall not reign over you. ***If there is among you a poor man of one of your brothers inside any of your gates in your land which the Lord your God Gives you, you shall not harden your heart, nor shut your hand from your poor brother; But you shall open your hand wide to him, and shall surely lend him sufficient for his need, in that which he lacks.***

There is a point to this Portion of the Bible. There shall be no poor among you... Why? It's because of generosity! Those that have means will share with the poor then there will no longer be any who are poor. Yet our Sages place a limit on how much a wealthy individual can give. Why? If a wealthy individual gives all they have then they have nothing. We are discussing an overall system of good. A few who are wealthy cannot accomplish what Ha Torah is requiring. For poverty to be vanquished it will require everyone's generosity. Dear Reader, each of us have a part to do. Stewardship is a responsibility for each of us. Stewardship does not mean the wealthy are responsible for every debt the poor make. It means they provide, they help with the necessities of life that one may not be able to provide. Necessities are indispensable NEEDS!!

It might be nice to have steak or fried chicken but the necessities are not steak or chicken. The necessities are good nutritious food that one can eat to live. Necessities may not be an auto for transportation but maybe a bus pass. Those who are not wealthy also have a responsibility to be careful with their funds. The burden should NOT be on the wealthy alone. There are some individuals who have very little yet each month they pay their bills. They don't eat steak. They enjoy some chicken. They are real careful with the limited funds they have. Yet each month they have extra. The reason they may have extra is because they have learned to be good Stewards. They may have extra because the Lord Has Blessed them. Regardless, just as the wealthy they are also responsible to assist the poor. They do this by sharing / teaching good management skills. And they do this by sharing some of what is left over. One is NOT to HOARD all that is left over each month. One may select who they can share money with. One may select good organizations that have proved to be excellent stewards with gifts over the years. In other words, one should Not be unwilling to give or to spend... Each of us should work and plan to arrive at a place of freedom and financial stability.

Stinginess is sometimes clothed in the desire to be practical. Many left over items can be used for a variety of good purposes. HOWEVER - Ask yourself this question. What materials was the Bet Ha Mikdash / The Holy Temple constructed from? What were the materials the Mishkan were constructed of? There is a principle here. If one has the means they should pay tithes. Do they pay their tithes first or last? Do they pay their tithes after all the bills have been paid? Again, this is the principle difference between Kayin's Tribute and Hevel's Tribute. Our Sages Teach that Kayin offered spoiled flax seed as his offering. Rabbi Meir Zlotowitz and Rabbi Nosson Scherman, The Artscroll Tanach Series - Bereishis Vol. I(a) (Brooklyn, New York: Mesorah Publications, Ltd. 3rd Impression, 1989), p 144

It was the last, poorest and worst instead the first, greatest and the best. Kayin was NOT opening his hand. Kayin was not giving anything of value. The scraps of his spoiled flaxseed were nothing to him. He had no plan for them.

Another meaning for the root Word of וּמֵחֶלְבֵהֶן Voo - May Cheh Lih Vay Hehn is Cheh Lev meaning milk. However it is not just milk it is the fat from the milk. It is the cream. Hevel gave the very best and Kayin the very worst. In Judaism the concept of opening one's hand to assist the poor is an obligation. Other religions teach their followers to be generous.

The generous are beckoned to Come, You, the generous are blessed of the Father. You will inherit a kingdom prepared for you from the foundation of the world. I was hungry and you gave me meat. I was thirsty, and you gave me drink: I was a stranger, and you took me in. I was naked, and you clothed me. I was sick, and you visited me. I was in prison, and you came to me. Then the righteous asked when? The King responded, When you help the least of these it is as if you did it to me...

The point is clear. Kayin would not give to help others because he did not give a proper Tribute to the Creator. This was a sin.

In the minds of some the misgiving that these were offerings may linger. This is understandable with all the religious teachings / doctrines in this area. Another point will help settle this.

As noted before the Word מִנְחָה Minchah is translated as offering. This is not entirely wrong but close. Using offering is wrong if you get the impression of an animal sacrifice because this Minchah is a present, a gift a tribute to our Creator. The second time (Genesis 32.14) and the third time (Genesis 32.19) Minchah is used is NOT translated offering but Tribute. The third time Minchah is used it is translated either as an offering or as a present.

Bereisheit 43.11

וַיֹּאמֶר אֲלֵהֶם יִשְׂרָאֵל אֲבִיהֶם אִם־כֵּן | אֵפוֹא זֹאת עֲשׂוּ קְחוּ מִזִּמְרַת הָאָרֶץ בִּכְלֵיכֶם וְהוֹרִידוּ לָאִישׁ **מִנְחָה** מְעַט צֳרִי וּמְעַט דְּבַשׁ נְכֹאת וָלֹט בָּטְנִים וּשְׁקֵדִים :

Genesis 43.11

And their father Israel said to them, If it must be so now, do this; take of the best fruits in the land in your utensils, and carry **down a present [.i.e. an offering]** *to the man, a little balm, and a little honey, spices, and myrrh, nuts, and almonds;*

There is no usage of Minchah in Exodus. Then the first two usages in Leviticus are Karbon Minchah, i.e. 'A Meal Offering'.

Vayikra 2.1

וְנֶפֶשׁ כִּי־תַקְרִיב **קָרְבַּן מִנְחָה** לַיהוָה סֹלֶת יִהְיֶה קָרְבָּנוֹ וְיָצַק עָלֶיהָ שֶׁמֶן וְנָתַן עָלֶיהָ לְבֹנָה:

Leviticus 2.1

And when any will offer a **meal offering** *to the Lord, his offering shall be of fine flour; and he shall pour oil upon it, and put frankincense on it;*

Vayikra 2.5

וְכִי תַקְרִב **קָרְבַּן מִנְחָה** מַאֲפֵה תַנּוּר סֹלֶת חַלּוֹת מַצֹּת בְּלוּלֹת בַּשֶּׁמֶן וּרְקִיקֵי מַצּוֹת מְשֻׁחִים בַּשָּׁמֶן: 1

Leviticus 2.4

And if you bring a sacrifice of **a meal offering** *baked in the oven, it shall be unleavened cakes of fine flour mixed with oil, or unleavened wafers anointed with oil.*

The point here is that when the Word Minchah is used in Leviticus the intent as an offering is clearly spelled out. It not left open to interpretation as in Genesis 4.3-5. In addition the Minchah Offering is NOT an animal offering. It is a meal offering as noted in Leviticus and in addition is offered upon an alter. In Genesis 4.3-5 there is no mention of an Altar. In fact NO WHERE is there a mention of an Altar or sacrifice in Genesis until after the Noach Flood in 1656 F.C. / From Creation - See Genesis 8.2.

It may be a little complicated to understand that our Creator did not permit the taking of animal life until after the flood. In Genesis 9.3 God Gives humankind the right to take the life of animals. Prior to this humankind was prohibited from taking any life for any reason. Was it after the flood that our Creator was concerned that grains, roots, berry, fruits and vegetables would not be enough to sustain man? No! Why then did God permit humankind to eat meat? What was the purpose of eating meat?

First, Our Sages Teach that after Noach and his sons cared for all the animals on the ark they had a right to receive some pleasure from the fruits of their labor.

Psalms 128.2
For you shall eat the labor of your hands; happy shall you be, and it shall be well with you.

Prior to this the Creator provided food for all animals. However, Noach and his family helped to provide food for the animals on the ark so our Creator gave humankind permission to enjoy the fruit of their labors. They cut the food, stored the food and fed the animals. Rabbi Nosson Scherman, The Stone Edition The Chumash (Mesorah Publications, Ltd., Brooklyn, N.Y. 1993), p. 351

First it was to provide man with a choice. What type of choice? When Noah entered into the Tava / the Ark he was instructed to take seven pairs of clean animals and birds and of unclean animals and birds only one pair. Why?

Bereisheit 7.2, 3

מִכֹּל **הַבְּהֵמָה הַטְּהוֹרָה** תִּקַּח־לְךָ שִׁבְעָה שִׁבְעָה אִישׁ וְאִשְׁתּוֹ וּמִן־הַבְּהֵמָה אֲשֶׁר לֹא טְהֹרָה הִוא שְׁנַיִם אִישׁ

וְאִשְׁתּוֹ :
גַּם מֵעוֹף הַשָּׁמַיִם שִׁבְעָה שִׁבְעָה זָכָר וּנְקֵבָה לְחַיּוֹת
זֶרַע עַל־פְּנֵי כָל־הָאָרֶץ:

Genesis 7.2, 3

*Of every **clean beast** you shall take to you seven pairs, the male and his female; and of beasts that are **not clean one pair**, the male and his female. Also, of birds of the air **by seven pairs**, the male and the female; to keep seed alive upon the face of all the earth.*

Our Creator Distinguished between clean animals and birds from unclean animals and birds. Our Creator Provided a greater abundance of clean animals and birds. There is a reason. Why did our Creator provide seven times as many clean animals and birds? It is to provide us with a choice between clean and unclean. It is also to give us a sign as to the type of animal one should choose. If one were to take the life of an animal which should he / she choose the clean or the unclean? The choice is obvious. The Lord wants us to choose the clean, i.e. the pure animals and birds. This is why the Lord required Noach to bring seven times more clean animals than unclean.

Our Creator's Intent does not have to do with humankind requiring more protein. We know that grains, roots, berries, fruits and vegetables are more than enough to sustain humankind. So what was the purpose of permitting clean and unclean, pure and not pure animals and birds? The Lord's Intent according to Pirkei d'Rabbi Eliezer was to provide animals and birds to humankind should they desire to bring offerings, Rabbi Nosson Scherman, The Stone Edition The Chumash (Mesorah Publications, Ltd., Brooklyn, N.Y. 1993), p. 39.

Second, being permitted to enjoy kosher animals was a result of Noach's righteousness and perfection.

Genesis 6.9
Noach was a righteous man perfect in his generations.

Note that through one righteous and perfect man

the world was saved, reestablished and humankind were permitted to eat Clean, Pure Kosher animals. Yes, I said ONLY KOSHER!! Our Creator taught Noach regarding the purpose of Clean and unclean animals.

Genesis 7.2,3
Of every clean beast you shall take to you seven pairs, the male and his female; and of beasts that are not clean one pair, the male and his female. [Do the same with the] birds of the air by seven pairs, the male and the female; to keep seed alive upon the face of all the earth.

Do you see this? *'to keep seed alive upon the face of the earth.'* The purpose was for humankind to choose clean animals and birds over unclean. The purpose was for us to offer sacrifices to The Lord. Had Noach and his children ate unclean animals there would be none left on the earth. READ BETWEEN THE LINES!! If Noach or if any of Noach's descendants were to eat just the male pig how would the pig propagate. The point is that they ate only clean animals and birds. This was established right here in Ha Torah as a Noachide custom. Want more proof? Why are there Clean and unclean animals and birds etc? The answer is Holiness! We are taught to separate the Holy from the unholy! We are permitted to ONLY offer the Holy to our Creator as a sacrifice. Please do not say to me that our Creator permitted the eating of non Holy animals to Noach and his children. OUR CREATOR PRESENTED THE CHOICE!!

Bereisheit 9.3

כָּל־רֶ֫מֶשׂ אֲשֶׁ֣ר הוּא־חַ֔י לָכֶ֥ם יִהְיֶ֖ה לְאָכְלָ֑ה כְּיֶ֣רֶק עֵ֔שֶׂב נָתַ֥תִּי לָכֶ֖ם אֶת־כֹּֽל׃

Genesis 9.3

All moving things with life may be consumed like [you consume] green herbs. I Have Given to you everything from the Letter Aleph to the Letter Tav [to consume].

Our Creator Gave the survivors of the flood the option to eat everything, even bugs. Our Creator in essence permitted us to choose between

Clean and unclean. Yet our Creator Taught Noach which animals and birds to take.

Bereisheit 7.2

מִכֹּל ׀ הַבְּהֵמָה הַטְּהוֹרָה תִּקַּח־לְךָ שִׁבְעָה שִׁבְעָה אִישׁ וְאִשְׁתּוֹ וּמִן־הַבְּהֵמָה אֲשֶׁר לֹא טְהֹרָה הִוא שְׁנַיִם אִישׁ וְאִשְׁתּוֹ :

Genesis 7.2

Of every clean beast you shall take to you seven pairs, the male and his female; and of beasts that are not clean one pair, the male and his female.

Notice the Words, תִּקַּח־לְךָ Tee Kah Ach - Lih Kaw meaning, 'You Shall Take'. So in Genesis 9.3 all animals, etc., are given to the survivors of the flood yet **Noach and his family were taught which animals to take.** They have a choice to take הַטְּהוֹרָה Ha- Tih Hoh Raw meaning, the Clean the purified, the unalloyed, the unadulterated, the unblemished, the immaculate animals birds etc as Commanded by God or to eat unclean

Notice the Words, לֹא טְהֹרָה Loh Tih Hoh Raw

meaning, NONE That Are to be CLEANSED!'. So we have the choice to take and to not take. Ha Torah Clearly Says! No Unclean! This is also a matter of common sense. Dear Readers, both words have a connection to clean. Some animals and birds are Clean. Some animals and birds are NOT clean.

הַטְהוֹרָה

Ha- Tih Hoh Raw meaning, the Clean the purified, the unalloyed, the unadulterated, the unblemished, the immaculate animals birds etc as Commanded by God.

טְהֹרָה

Tih Hoh Raw meaning, NONE That Are to be CLEANSED!' The Letter Vav is removed from the the second. Why is this significant? It is because the Letter Vav is a connecting Letter. **Mystically, this Teaches us we are to be connected to the Clean the purified, the unalloyed, the unadulterated, the unblemished, the immaculate animals, birds, etc., that Our Creator Commanded us to take.** When one reads and understands that the Word טְהֹרָה only has to do with the cleansing process, and in comparison to the actual state of true purity. Now one must simply ask, do I want to do what God Commanded? Do I want to bring Spirituality into my life? Do I want to be among those desiring to be completely pure?

Now we have taken quite a trip discussing the difference between a Gift... A Tribute and an Offering to the Lord God and what is Kosher and Clean and Pure from what is not. It is now time for us to return to Leviticus.

God did NOT Command us to eat meat. The Lord Gave us the opportunity to bring sacrifices to Him and as a result to enjoy parts of the meat or fowl after it was offered on the altar. The intent was not to set up slaughter houses and butcher shops to sell meat for our wood burning grills. Our world has wandered so far from the intent of offerings.

The purpose for sacrifices was to teach us that there is a Being, the Lord God, Who is greater than mankind that the Karbon is offered to.
The purpose was to teach us to return to the

place of our formation, to the place where we were drawn from the dust of the earth where the Creator Gave us physical form and the Spirit of Life where the Lord God formed Adam and Eve.

The purpose was to teach us only certain animals can be an offering. Only the clean / pure animals may be used as sacrifices. When a pure animal or bird is offered to our Creator the Soul of that animal or bird is elevated providing it is offered correctly.

Our Creator Gave Noachides / non-Jews instructions about offerings. Here in Leviticus our Creator Expands on the directions given to Noachides about offerings. One of the very important instructions given to Noachides was to remove blood from the animal or bird. We will discuss this now.

Genesis 9.3 - 5
Every moving thing that lives shall be food for you; even as the green herb have I Given you all things. **_But_** *flesh with its life, which is its blood, you shall not eat. And surely*

your blood of your lives will I require; at the hand of every beast will I require it, and at the hand of man; at the hand of every man's brother will I require the life of man.

We learn that Noachides are NOT to consume blood. Jews are not to consume blood either. Any teaching rather literal or symbolic that teaches one to consume blood is incorrect! The Life... the Soul... the Spirit... the Breath is in the blood.

Here in Leviticus we learn that one MUST own the offering. The offering must not be stolen or borrowed!! Now, when we are speaking about the Tabernacle there is a 2,448 year span between Adam and The People of Israel. However, B'nai Noach / the Children of Noach were permitted to eat meat and poultry only during the last 791 years from when the flood ended. There was a wandering away from the purpose of eating meat. There was a wandering away from the altar where the sacrifice was made. So our Creator selected B'nei Yisroel / The People of Israel to bring back the purpose for offerings. Offerings are to draw our attention to God. After B'nei Yisroel worshipped the golden calf our Creator selected the Tribe of Levi to be the representatives in the Mishkon area. Aaron and his sons and their descendants were selected to offer sacrifices to our Creator in behalf of B'nei Yisroel and everyone else. They are the Kohanim / Priests. One of the responsibilities of the Kohanim is to follow the correct pattern for offering the Karbon. Our Creator Appointed the Levites to assist the Priests in and around the Tabernacle area.

This leads us to discussing 'ORDER' and 'PROCEDURE'. Here we consider God's Prescribed instructions for offering a Karbon. This brings us to Leviticus. When we leave Leviticus we learn that pagans destroyed our first Temple. We rebuilt the Holy Temple. Sacrifice resumed. Pagans destroyed the second Holy Temple. Sacrifices have not resumed. We pray daily for the rebuilding of our Holy Temple and the resumption of Sacrifices.

From Creation certain animals and birds were

intended specifiably as sacrifices. They are born and raised with this intention in mind. In a sense animals are elevated above other animals like the Levites and Priests are elevated above the People of Israel. There are animals and birds and then there are animals and birds that may be offered as sacrifices then there is the red heifer. Each is at a higher level of sanctification. A story in the Talmud helps to explain this.

Our Rabbis say: Once the Sages came to him to Askelon, where he lived, to buy from him a precious stone [to replace one] lost from the vestments of the [High] Priest, and they fixed the price with him at a thousand golden pieces. He entered the house and found his father asleep with his leg stretched out on the chest wherein the stone was lying. He would not trouble him, and he came out empty-handed. As he did not produce the stone the Sages thought that he wanted a higher price, and they therefore raised their offer to ten thousand golden pieces. When his father awoke from his sleep Dama entered and brought out the stone. The Sages wished to give him ten thousand golden pieces, but he

exclaimed: 'Heaven forfend! I will not make a profit out of honoring my parents; I will only take from you the first price, one thousand golden pieces, which I had fixed with you.' And what reward did the Holy One, blessed be He, give him? Our Rabbis report that in the very same year his cow gave birth to a red heifer which he sold for more than ten thousand golden pieces.
Devarim Rabba 1.15

We learn from this story that honoring one's parent is very important.. When we are taught to honor our parents we learn to honor our Creator.

How important is the Red Heifer? We are looking forward to the time when the Third Holy Temple will be rebuilt. We are looking forward to ritual animal sacrifices in the Holy Temple. However, they cannot begin without purification rituals which require the ashes from the Red Heifer. The Red Heifer is part of a very important purification procedure. Without the offering of the Red Heifer individuals with certain types of impurities will not be purified. They can only be purified through a special ash mixture. Without this purification they cannot enter the Holy Temple. Who wants to be locked outside the Holy Temple?

Another Order and Procedure is the Priestly Meal Offering by the High Priest. He offers the Priestly Meal Offering when he becomes the High Priest then he offers the Priestly Meal Offering daily each morning and each afternoon everyday for the rest of his life.

Why I am sharing this? Dear Reader, there is a process established by our Creator regarding offerings and sacrifices. This is an important process. This is an eternal process. The process must be followed. Some individuals can afford to offer cattle others a sheep or a goat from their flocks and others turtledoves or young pigeons. The procedure for offering these is discussed in chapter one. However it does not end here. Chapter two begins with offering a meal offering for atonement for those who cannot afford animals, flocks or birds. The entire chapter explains how to offer a meal offering for atonement to the Lord. In Exodus 30. we learn that money is an atonement for our souls.

Exodus 30.12-16

*When you take the census of the people of Israel according to their number, then shall **they give every man a ransom for his soul to the Lord,** when you count them; that there should be no plague among them, when you count them. This they shall give, every one who passes among those who are counted, half a shekel according to the shekel of the sanctuary; a shekel is twenty gerahs; a half shekel shall be the offering of the Lord. Every one who passes among those who are counted, from twenty years old and above, shall give an offering to the Lord. The rich shall not give more, and the poor shall not give less than half a shekel, **when they give an offering to the Lord, to make an atonement for your souls. And you shall take the atonement money of The People of Israel,** and shall appoint it for the service of the Tent of Meeting; that **it may be a memorial to the people of Israel before the Lord, to make an atonement for your souls.**

In addition David Wrote in Psalms 51, *'The sacrifices of God are a broken spirit; a broken and contrite heart, O God, you will not despise.'*
Later, we read that blood makes an an atonement for our souls. This is true to a degree. What do I mean? We go back to the procedure. Was the correct procedure followed? If an animal is stolen this is a violation of the procedure. One will not receive atonement from an animal that does not lawfully belong to him. We learn from the Wording in Leviticus 1.2.

Vayikra 1.2

דַּבֵּר אֶל־בְּנֵי יִשְׂרָאֵל וְאָמַרְתָּ אֲלֵהֶם **אָדָם** כִּי־יַקְרִיב מִכֶּם קׇרְבָּן לַיהוָה מִן־הַבְּהֵמָה מִן־הַבָּקָר וּמִן־הַצֹּאן תַּקְרִיבוּ אֶת־קׇרְבַּנְכֶם׃

Leviticus 1.2

Speak to The People of Israel, and say to them, **If any man** *of you brings an offering to the Lord, you shall bring your offering of the cattle, of the herd, and of the flock.*

The Torah Portion of the Hebrew Bible Says, If אָדָם Adam brings and offering... We must inquire, why then do we translate this passage as *'if any man brings an offering'?* Our Sages Instruct that the reason is The Creator Gave all animals to Adam. Therefore one cannot bring an animal that does not belong to him. If one were to offer a stolen animal as an offering, the blood of that animal would not atone. If the grass or grain the animal fed from were stolen, the blood would not atone. If the animal had a blemish, the blood would not atone. Why do I mention this? The correct procedure was NOT followed and therefore the blood does not atone.

Human blood cannot atone!! The ONLY blood that can atone is that from a kosher animal. Where in Ha Torah do we read that human blood atones for sins? Ha Torah does not say anything to this effect!! **The procedures of Ha Torah MUST be followed!**

Ha Torah also Says one may not offer the blood of my sacrifice with leavened bread. This means the offering cannot be defined with sin.

The fat from the offering cannot be left on the altar overnight. Exodus 23.18 Dear Reader, these are procedures that must be followed otherwise the atonement blood is void.

Let's discuss how important the procedure is. Say, for example, even though The Lord God Commanded that the blood from the Passover Offering be placed on the door post by hyssop from the passover offering that one used a palm branch instead hyssop or that one hung a bloody rag above the door or that one placed the blood inside the house. Etc.. would the firstborn be spared? No!

Exodus 12.23
For the Lord will pass through to strike the Egyptians; and when he sees the blood upon the lintel, and on the two side posts, the Lord will pass over the door, and will not let the destroyer come into your houses to strike you.

Procedure is important in these matters. Ha Torah Says the location of the offering is important, 'If a man brings... his offering to the door of the Tent of Meeting... in Leviticus 1.3 and later to the Temple courtyard. A blood offering that is not offered according to procedure is void. The offering does not atone. Now Leviticus 17.11 Says the life of the flesh is in the blood and that blood makes atonement for the soul. Let's read Leviticus 17.11.

Vayikra 17.11

כִּי־נֶפֶשׁ הַבָּשָׂר בַּדָּם הוּא וַאֲנִי נְתַתִּיו לָכֶם עַל־הַמִּזְבֵּחַ לְכַפֵּר עַל־נַפְשֹׁתֵיכֶם כִּי־הַדָּם הוּא בַּנֶּפֶשׁ יְכַפֵּר׃

Leviticus 17.11
For the soul of the flesh is in the blood; and I have given it to you upon the altar to makes atonement for your souls; for the blood that makes atonement for the soul.

The Bible does not Say 'LIFE' ! Why? Because our life is dependent upon blood.

Vayikra 17.11

כִּי־נֶפֶשׁ הַבָּשָׂר בַּדָּם הוּא וַאֲנִי נְתַתִּיו לָכֶם עַל־הַמִּזְבֵּחַ לְכַפֵּר עַל־נַפְשֹׁתֵיכֶם כִּי־הַדָּם הוּא בַּנֶּפֶשׁ יְכַפֵּר׃

Leviticus 17.11
For the soul of the flesh is in the blood; **and**

I have given it to you upon the altar to makes atonement for your souls; for the blood that makes atonement for the soul.

לְכַפֵּר עַל־נַפְשֹׁתֵיכֶם
To ATONE FOR YOUR SOULS...
The Blood of animals and birds, etc., does not just cover sin as some teach. Blood ATONES for sin!

Vayikra 17.11

כִּי־נֶפֶשׁ הַבָּשָׂר בַּדָּם הִוא וַאֲנִי נְתַתִּיו לָכֶם עַל־הַמִּזְבֵּחַ לְכַפֵּר עַל־נַפְשֹׁתֵיכֶם כִּי־הַדָּם הוּא בַּנֶּפֶשׁ יְכַפֵּר:

Leviticus 17.11
For the soul of the flesh is in the blood; and I have given it to you upon the altar to make an atonement for your souls; **for the blood [from animals and birds] makes atonement for the soul.**

Blood from animals makes atonement for our souls as well as money and unleavened bread as already noted. **This Verse does NOT say ONLY Blood makes atonement for your souls**. The

Verse Says *blood [from animals and birds] makes atonement for the soul.* **And as a result we are taught NOT to consume blood!**

Vayikra 7.26

וְכָל־דָּם לֹא תֹאכְלוּ בְּכֹל מוֹשְׁבֹתֵיכֶם לָעוֹף וְלַבְּהֵמָה׃

Leviticus 7.26
And you shall not consume any kind of blood, *whether it is of bird or of beast, in any of your dwellings.*

Vayikra 17.10

וְאִישׁ אִישׁ מִבֵּית יִשְׂרָאֵל וּמִן־הַגֵּר הַגָּר בְּתוֹכָם אֲשֶׁר יֹאכַל **כָּל־דָּם** וְנָתַתִּי פָנַי בַּנֶּפֶשׁ הָאֹכֶלֶת **אֶת־הַדָּם** וְהִכְרַתִּי אֹתָהּ מִקֶּרֶב עַמָּהּ׃

Leviticus 17.10
Men, [in general] and Men from the house of Israel and from the converts and the strangers among them that consumes **ANY BLOOD** *and I will set my face on the soul who consumes* **anything from The Letter Aleph to The Letter Tav of blood,** *and I Will cut that one off from the midst of its people.*

One should NOT symbolically consume blood either since it is a Serious Sin to consume blood. One should NOT say to others, Here is a cup of wine. It is symbolically my blood. Take it and drink it... This is a sin taught by other religions.

And Jesus took the cup of wine and gave thanks and gave it to his followers and said 'Drink all of it for this is symbolically my blood...' Matthew 26.26-27.

Ha Torah Has a serious problem with Jewish congregations who openly welcome violators of this Mitzvot of Ha Torah to participate and be members of their congregation. They openly and blatantly define Pesach with the above described act of symbolically consuming blood. Does anyone wonder why Moshiach has not come with such despicable acts going on in some Jewish homes.

Blood from cattle, goats, sheep and birds can atone for us when all the procedures are followed. **Human blood cannot atone for anything!!**

A Karbon Offering is slaughtered before The Lord, before the Kohen Godal and the Kohanim on the Temple grounds, NOT as a prisoner in a Roman prison or prison guards. Then the Karbon's blood is sprinkled around a very holy place, the Mez Bay Ach, the altar. The Karbon is skinned and cut into pieces then the pieces are arranged in a certain order upon the altar and burnt. The innards and the legs are washed, then burned upon the altar.

Our God is a very loving God! Our God considers the Karbon / Offering needs of all His people. God has provided a way for each of us to offer a Karbon even if it's only a handful of flour or our Tefillah, that is, our prayers. **Our offerings are between each of us and The Lord our God!**

Today we, the Jewish people live in a time saddened by the loss of our Holy Temple. Jews are scattered throughout the world. We live in the diaspora. We, the Jewish people have no Temple yet **ALL our sins are forgiven** and atoned for if we acknowledge our error, make a plan to not repeat our error and are willing to pay restitution.

Each of us has both a physical Mishkon / Tabernacle and a spiritual Mishkon / Tabernacle. '...Our Sages consider this {the Mishkon} to mean dwelling places {tents} of learning and prayer, the Jewish home, the Jewish neshama where God presently resides in the absence of the Beit HaMikdosh / The Holy Temple. So the first step in lifting up the third Holy Temple as in the wilderness 'Echad Mishkon' is the restoration of each Jewish soul and of each Jewish home with learning and prayer. This is the responsibility of every Jew everywhere! The Mishkon cannot be restored without you. As the Miami Boys Choir sings, 'We need your Tefillah.' We, Kal Yisroel, are Ha Mishkon Echad!

Now, dear readers, we see this connection in the statement, *when a soul [meaning person] brings a meal offering....* Our Sages say the usage of 'Nefesh' meaning soul is in reference to a poor person that cannot afford an animal or bird offering. It is God's way of making it possible for that person to give an offering to The Lord. Dear Reader, just as God Made a way for the poorest individuals to give a Karbon, God has also made a way for every Jew living in the diaspora to offer sacrifices to Him as well as every Noachide!

The Karbon that we can offer to The Lord is from the Temple grounds of our nefesh, of our soul. Our Sages expounded on the concept that a poor person actually gives their soul for sacrifice to The Lord. How? The poor person offers a matzoh as a Karbon to The Lord. The matzoh is unleavened bread. It has no yeast! It has no sin. Yet the message behind the matzoh is, *'By the sweat of your brow shall you eat bread,'* Genesis 3.9. That being the situation Adam, the first man, had to labor hard to offer matzoh to The Lord. Each of us has to labor very hard to offer matzoh as a sacrifice to The Lord. We have to prepare fields, plow fields, sow fields, reap fields, stack, thresh, winnow, clean, grind, sift, build an oven, gather wood to heat the oven, create and prepare a mixing bowl, gather olives for oil, mix and bake the matzoh. When we gather the olives for oil, it is necessary to climb the olive tree and dangle from the branches. This is dangerous. We could fall and be killed from the fall, God forbid! In doing all this labor and in placing our life at risk, it is as if we actually offer our soul to The Lord when we give the matzoh.

Then when we offer the matzoh it is not like we experience the same effects as placing our hand on an animal's forehead, cutting the animal's throat, watching it bleed, watching the animal's blood being gathered and sprinkled before the altar, watching as the animal is cut into pieces and arranged on the altar, watching as the innards and legs are washed and burnt on the altar. Offering matzoh does not have this effect. Why?

When a soul offers matzoh, that soul is required to prepare before offering the matzoh to The Lord. This is not by accident because this Teaches us what to do in the absence of an animal Karbon. This Teaches us what to do in the absence of the Beit Ha Mikdosh. This is what we do today. This is the procedure for times like these. This is how we offer to The Lord now! Rabbi Zalman Sorotzkin states, that one should examine his / her deeds. One should think deeply. One should ask him / her self is it fitting to offer a meal offering to the One Who said:

Malachi 1.11
From the rising of the sun to its going down, My Name is great among the nations, and in every place burnt offerings are presented to My Name, and pure meal-offerings.

Dear Reader, if the nations of the world offer 'pure meal-offerings' to The Lord, then B'nei Yisroel should also. As a result one should feel the necessity to contemplate whether his meal-offering is offered with purity. One should ask, am I pure. Am I holy?

Malachi 1.10 – Adapted from Drusius / Maurer
Would that there was absolutely someone who would shut the doors of the Temple (which is in the inner court, where the altar of Burnt Offerings is), and that you would not kindle fire on My altar in vain! The thought is, better no sacrifice

offerings than vain sacrifice offerings.

In other words do not contaminate the offering with impure deeds. Malachi is saying that the Lord does not want a meal-offering from your hands. Who is capable of making such an important introspection? I am not! Are you? This type of introspection can only be accomplished by an individual who is in control of his own soul. Therefore the verse says: 'When a *soul* offers a meal-offering...'

Dear Reader, in the exact same way we are to offer Tefillah from the Mishkon of our pure Nefesh / Soul. In other words we are to clean and maintain our Soul, the heart of the Mishkon within us so we do have a Spiritual place from which to offer the Karbon of praise to The Lord. David Said,

Tehillim 51.17 - 19

אֲדֹנָי שְׂפָתַי תִּפְתָּח וּפִי יַגִּיד תְּהִלָּתֶךָ:
כִּי ׀ לֹא־תַחְפֹּץ זֶבַח וְאֶתֵּנָה עוֹלָה לֹא תִרְצֶה:
זִבְחֵי אֱלֹהִים רוּחַ נִשְׁבָּרָה לֵב־נִשְׁבָּר וְנִדְכֶּה אֱלֹהִים לֹא תִבְזֶה:

Psalms 51.17 - 19 / KJV - Psalms 51.15 - 17

'Oh Lord open my lips that my mouth may declare Your Praise. For You do not desire **a sacrifice,** *else I would give it;* **a burnt offering** *You do not want.* **The Sacrifices God Desires** *are a broken Spirit; a heart broken and humbled, Oh God, You will not despise...'*

David uses the Words תְּהִלָּתֶךָ Tih Hee Law Taw Caw meaning 'Your Praises', זֶבַח Zaw Vah Ach meaning animal sacrifices and עוֹלָה Oh Lawh meaning Burnt Offerings that rises upwards to The Lord God in the Heavens. Understanding the difference between these three Words is crucial to knowing The Truth.

Bereisheit 31.54

וַיִּזְבַּח יַעֲקֹב זֶבַח בָּהָר וַיִּקְרָא לְאֶחָיו לֶאֱכָל־לָחֶם וַיֹּאכְלוּ לֶחֶם וַיָּלִינוּ בָּהָר׃

Genesis 31.54

And He, Yaakov / Jacob Sacrificed, **a sacrifice** *upon the mount. And He Called his brothers to eat bread; and they ate bread, and stayed all night in the mount.*

When Kayin and Hevel brought a tribute to The Lord in Genesis 4.3 - 5 these three Words were NOT USED!! The Word used for their Tribute to The Lord was Minchah. It was NOT Zaw Vah Ach meaning animal sacrifices!! It was NOT עוֹלָה Oh Lawh meaning Burnt Offerings that rises upwards to The Lord God in the Heavens. Their Tribute was NOT a blood sacrifice as certain religions falsely proclaim.

We return to David's comments. Each time before we begin praying the Amidah each morning, afternoon and evening we say, *"O Lord open my lips that my mouth may declare Your praise."* Our Praises to The Lord God are not a Minchah Tribute or זֶבַח בָּ a Zaw Vah Ach / animal sacrifices or עוֹלָה a Oh Lawh / Burnt Offering. Our Praises are the daily Tefilliah that we offer to The Lord God from the Mishkon of our Nefesh, i.e. our Soul.

In Leviticus 1.1-5 we note that the Word קָרְבָּן Kaw Rih Bawn means 'Offering'. Kayin and Hevel did not bring a קָרְבָּן Kaw Rih Bawn to The Lord. The Word קָרְבָּן Kaw Rih Bawn is NOT used in

Genesis 4.3 - 5. Yet many translators incorrectly say they brought an offering to The Lord. Kayin and Hevel brought a Tribute to The Lord. It is for reasons like this that translators MUST be so very careful because one incorrect translation can give the wrong impression!! The jump from Offering to Sacrifice is easy to make. The jump from Tribute to Sacrifice is not. This is how misunderstandings begin. This is how pseudo doctrines begin.

We began by saying,

Vayikra 1.1 – 5.26

וַיִּקְרָא אֶל־מֹשֶׁה וַיְדַבֵּר יְהוָה אֵלָיו מֵאֹהֶל מוֹעֵד לֵאמֹר: דַּבֵּר אֶל־בְּנֵי יִשְׂרָאֵל וְאָמַרְתָּ אֲלֵהֶם **אָדָם כִּי־יַקְרִיב** מִכֶּם **קָרְבָּן לַיהוָה מִן־**הַבְּהֵמָה **מִן־הַבָּקָר** וּמִן־הַצֹּאן תַּקְרִיבוּ אֶת־קָרְבַּנְכֶם:

Leviticus 1.1 – 5.26

And He Called to Moses, and the Lord Said, to him from the Tent of Witness Saying, Speak to the People of Israel and say to them **[if Adam]** *If a man among you brings* *an Offering to the Lord from animals, from the cattle, and from the sheep you shall bring everything from Aleph to Tav of your offering.*

אָדָם כִּי־יַקְרִיב
[if Adam] If a man among you brings...
397= 2ב 10י 200ר 100ק 10י 10י 20כ 40ם 4ד 1א

מִן־הַבָּקָר
From His Animals
397 = 200ר 100ק 2ב 5ה 50ן 40מ

Originally all the animals belonged to Adam. Our Sages point to Adam's ownership of all animals. Leviticus 1.2 is a reflection on Adam's ownership because it Says, '...*if Adam among you brings...*' We translate this is as '...*if a man among you brings...*' because we understand we must gain ownership of the animals from Adam. The second Gematria brings this point a little closer with the Words, 'From his animals'. Adam used to own the animals but now they are from some else's flock. The Torah Says 'from his animals'. This speaks of the ownership. Yet,

Adam offered matzah. He brought Unleavened Bread to the Lord as his Tribute.

In My book entitled *Would You Like To Be Jewish 2?* we discuss these important topics beginning around page 104 to the end of the book. I am going to borrow a few pages that discuss repentance. Why? Individuals who have believed sin can only be forgiven with a blood sacrifice may now be entangled in confusion because the Truth of Genesis 4.3 - 5 is being revealed. Lets return to what David Said.

Psalms 51.17 - 19 / KJV - Psalms 51.15 - 17
*'Oh Lord open my lips that my mouth may declare Your Praise. For You do not desire **a sacrifice,** else I would give it; **a burnt offering** You do not want. **The Sacrifices God Desires** are a broken Spirit; a heart broken and humbled, Oh God, You will not despise...'*

King David Said, 'For You do not desire a Sacrifice, else I would give it; a Burnt Offering You do not want. King David is specifically speaking about a Sacrifice for his sin. He is speaking about a Burnt Offering for his sin. Dear ones bringing a Sacrifice or a Burnt Offering does not eradicate one's sins. An individual may bring all the Sacrifices and Burnt Offerings they desire and they will NOT remove any sin if the individual is just going through a formality. Sin is forgiven by first being touched by what ones has done that is not correct... that is a mistake... that is an improper behavior... that is a sin... One has a broken Spirit. One realizes their Spirit is broken and needs repair. One is humbled by their improper action by their sin. Then one confesses their mistake to The Lord God, One makes a plan not to repeat their mistake, one offers restitution for their mistake. At this point the sinner is restored. Our Creator Instructed Kayin to simply 'IMPROVE'. David taught us to acknowledge our sins to The Lord God. David taught us to be humble, i.e. to confess our errors to The Lord God. This is how sins are forgiven. This is the basis for receiving forgiveness for sin. Now let's examine the basis for this Teaching from Ha Torah.

Genesis 4.3
And in process of time it came to pass, that

Cain brought of the fruit of the ground an Tribute to the Lord.

Kayin's Tribute was spoiled flax seed. Cain's Tribute was not accepted because it was not from the first fruit and because the Tribute was spoiled flax seed. It was slimy. It was not a Praise! It was not Homage. It was Not a Salute. It was an insult!! The Word מִנְחָה Minchah tells us the Tribute was not meat. The pseudo tribute was spoiled produce. Kayin's heart / Spirit was not right.

In Genesis 4.4 we review Abel's Tribute.

Bereisheit 4.4

וְהֶבֶל הֵבִיא גַם־הוּא מִבְּכֹרוֹת צֹאנוֹ וּמֵחֶלְבֵהֶן
וַיִּשַׁע יְהוָה אֶל־הֶבֶל וְאֶל־**מִנְחָתוֹ** :

Genesis 4.4
And Abel also brought of the firstlings of his flock and of rich cream of it. And the Lord had respect for Abel and for his ***offering;***

One could also say rich cream or the fat of the

Tribute because the spelling for rich cream and animal fat is the same. Yet we know it was not an animal sacrifice because the Word **Minchato** tells us this was a Tribute and therefore was not meat.

What did The Creator Say to Kayin?

The Creator Said, *'If you improve there is forgiveness..'* Genesis 4.7 So we see the plan to receive forgiveness is to simply 'Improve'. However, part of improving is acknowledging the mistake. Take ownership for doing wrong. Kayin would not take ownership for his sin. Therefore sin lay at his door and it consumed him. He died in his sins. He entered eternity in defiance to his sin. He perished!

Noach brought a 'Burnt Offering'. This is identified by the Word עלת Oh Loht which represents it was a bird or animal. When the Word Minchah is used it is not an animal. When the Word Oh Lam or Oh Loht are used it is an animal sacrifice.

Bereisheit 8.20

וַיִּבֶן נֹחַ מִזְבֵּחַ לַיהוָה וַיִּקַּח מִכֹּל
הַבְּהֵמָה הַטְּהֹרָה וּמִכֹּל הָעוֹף הַטָּהוֹר
וַיַּעַל **עֹלֹת** בַּמִּזְבֵּחַ:

Genesis 8.20

And Noah built an altar to the Lord; and took of every clean beast, and of every clean bird, and offered **burnt offerings** *on the altar.*

A Meal-Offering
מ40 נ50 ח8 ת400 = 498

In the second set of Gematria Relationships we observe the Gematria 498 is 'An offering to the Lord from... from what? The next word would be animal. However we already know it's from the animals or the birds. Yet we learn from the Gematria 498 it may also be a Meal-Offering. Mee Nih Chaht – meaning Meal Offering is the Gematria 498. Mystically this means if one were to bring to the Lord an offering that it may also be a Meal-Offering.

Vayikra 5.1

וְנֶ֣פֶשׁ כִּֽי־תֶחֱטָ֗א וְשָֽׁמְעָה֙ ק֣וֹל אָלָ֔ה וְה֣וּא עֵ֔ד א֥וֹ רָאָ֖ה א֣וֹ יָדָ֑ע אִם־ל֥וֹא יַגִּ֖יד וְנָשָׂ֥א עֲוֺנֽוֹ׃

Leviticus 5.1

*And if **a soul** sins, and hears the voice of swearing, and is a witness, whether he has seen or known of it; if he does not utter it, then he shall bear his iniquity.*

Bereisheit 46.27

וּבְנֵ֥י יוֹסֵ֛ף אֲשֶׁר־יֻלַּד־ל֥וֹ בְמִצְרַ֖יִם **נֶ֣פֶשׁ** שְׁנָ֑יִם כָּל־הַ**נֶּ֧פֶשׁ** לְבֵֽית־יַעֲקֹ֛ב הַבָּ֥אָה מִצְרַ֖יְמָה שִׁבְעִֽים׃

Genesis 46.27

*And the sons of Joseph, who were born to him in Egypt, were two **soul**[s]; all the **soul**[s] of the house of Jacob, who came to Egypt, were seventy.*

The point here is the word Soul is used when making reference to two souls and when making reference to seventy souls. two soul are 'One Soul'. Seventy Souls are 'One Soul' This Teaches that we are bound together. We are our brothers keeper. We share the same bond. We share the same soul. Notice Leviticus 5.1 uses the same Word נֶפֶשׁ Nefesh / Soul as Genesis 46.27. In Genesis 46.27 all seventy souls are called נֶפֶשׁ one single soul. In part this is why on Yom Kippur we plead for our sins the sins our one soul has committed. Our Creator groups us together as if we each shared the same soul. So when we say 'If a soul sins' we are speaking both on an individual basis and a community basis. If one is poor they may gain atonement with an offering of a tenth-ephah of flour. NO BLOOD!

If one takes a careful look at the writings in Hebrews which are part of The Christian Writings the following is stated:

Hebrews 9:22
And **almost** all things are by the law purged with blood; and without shedding of blood is no remission.

For whatever reason the 'ALMOST' is often missed... I have offered many examples where blood is not required to purge sin as discussed in this chapter. **Our concluding point is this our Creator has always had a plan for sin.** I discuss His plan in *Would You Like To Be Jewish 2?* The plan is simple. 'IMPROVE!' Our Creator's plan has nothing to do with a savior or murdering a man at Passover. We acknowledge our sin. We make a plan to change. We offer restitution. We improve. When we die we go to heaven. We do not need to worry about hell. Instead we should concern ourselves with Obedience. Judaism places the emphasis on a loving Creator who deeply cares about all His Creation. Everyone is important to the Lord. This is how salvation is received and maintained.

Living Separated
Chapter 2

Parshat Tzav
Leviticus 6.1 - 8.36

Vayikra 8.1-6

וַיְדַבֵּר יְהוָה אֶל־מֹשֶׁה לֵּאמֹר:
קַח אֶת־אַהֲרֹן וְאֶת־בָּנָיו אִתּוֹ וְאֵת הַבְּגָדִים וְאֵת שֶׁמֶן הַמִּשְׁחָה וְאֵת ׀ פַּר הַחַטָּאת וְאֵת שְׁנֵי הָאֵילִים וְאֵת סַל הַמַּצּוֹת:
וְאֵת כָּל־הָעֵדָה הַקְהֵל אֶל־פֶּתַח אֹהֶל מוֹעֵד:
וַיַּעַשׂ מֹשֶׁה כַּאֲשֶׁר צִוָּה יְהוָה אֹתוֹ וַתִּקָּהֵל הָעֵדָה אֶל־פֶּתַח אֹהֶל מוֹעֵד:
וַיֹּאמֶר מֹשֶׁה אֶל־הָעֵדָה זֶה הַדָּבָר אֲשֶׁר־צִוָּה יְהוָה לַעֲשׂוֹת:
וַיַּקְרֵב מֹשֶׁה אֶת־אַהֲרֹן וְאֶת־בָּנָיו וַיִּרְחַץ אֹתָם בַּמָּיִם:

Leviticus 8.1-6
And the Lord Spoke to Moses, Saying, Take Aaron and his sons with him, and the

garments, and the anointing oil, and a bull for the sin offering, and two rams, and a basket of unleavened bread; And gather all the Congregation together to the door of the Tent of Meeting / Tabernacle. And Moses did as the Lord Commanded him; and the assembly was gathered together to the door of the Tent of Meeting. And Moses Said to the congregation, This is the thing which the Lord Commanded to be done And he, Moses brought Everything from Aleph to Tav of Aharon and everything from Aleph to Tav of his sons and bathed them in water.

The word וַיַּקְרֵב Vah Yah Kih Rayv means to draw, to bring inward or to bring into the midst. The Congregation was assembled at the entrance to the Tent of Meeting. Then Moshe brought inward everything from Aleph to Tav of Aharon and everything from Aleph to Tav of the sons of Aharon. What we are reading is, Moshe SEPARATED Aharon and his sons from The People of Israel / from The People of Israel on the outside of the Tabernacle. He drew them into the midst of the Tent of Meeting. The

Presence of the Creator was there. All Yisroel was focused on the entrance to the Tabernacle. This is represented by the Gematria 318.

וַיִּקְרֵב
Vah Yah Kih Rayv
To draw, To bring inward, To bring into the midst
318 = ב2 ר200 ק100 י10 ו6

שׁוּבִי
Shoo Vee
To return to Torah Observance
To Obey the Commands of Ha Torah
318 = י10 ב2 ו6 ש300

In Chapter one we discussed the Holiness ' purity required **for the soul** of the one that would bring flour as an offering for sin. The power of purity and the power of Holiness had to be representative of the one who brought the flour. I stated it had to be from one's heart. Bringing the offering of flour had to be more that a formality. Our discussion in this Parshat is about the process for the High Priest and the Priests being drawn out from The People of Israel and into service in the Tent of Meeting. They had to be on a high level of Holiness to serve the Holy Soul that brings the offerings.

Feeling drawn into the midst of the Holy Tabernacle is not enough. One must Shoo Vee, i.e., Spiritually return. The Gematria for שׁוּבִי is 318.

Now our second point of focus is on the words אֶת־אַהֲרֹן וְאֶת־בָּנָיו Eht Aharon and Vi Eht Baw Nawv. These words inform us that Aharon and his sons were drawn entirely. They were brought to the fullest extent into the Tent of Meeting. He drew their personalities... The Lord God Drew their natures...The Lord God Drew their thought patterns... He Drew their Souls... He Drew their physical beings. He Drew everything about them into the center of the Tent of Meeting. Nothing about these men was left outside of the Tent of Meeting. Everything about them was making this commitment. Their entire beings were 100% drawn. It is basically impossible in words to express the entirety of their separation or of their being drawn. If one could find the words to express the entirety of their separation, still understanding their separation would be difficult.

In our age one cannot grasp the fullness... the extent... the entirety of such separation. Their separation was so deep and so committed that words like zealous evaporates into thin air. Their level of commitment to God, to Torah and to Observances has the rest of The People of Israel fastened to the entrance of the Tent of Meeting. All the People of Israel are focused on the entrance to the Tent of Meeting that Aharon, Ha Kohen Godal and his sons Ha Kohanim were just drawn into. The People of Israel is spellbound so to speak. In their midst something wonderful... powerful... incredible was happening that would change their lives and the world forever. B'nei Yisroel is witness to this powerful event. The Torah Portion of the Bible Says, וַיֹּאמֶר מֹשֶׁה אֶל־הָעֵדָה *'And He Moshe Said to the Congregation...'* Yet we could say this differently. *'And He Moshe Said to the Witness...'* This is also an accepted and appropriate translation. Like in Chapter One where we discussed the Word Nefesh. i.e. the souls of 70 people being just One Soul. Here we have several million people witnessing this important event through one single eye. The Torah Says, 'The Witness'. **B'nai Yisroel saw the event in unity, as one.**

Point Three is acceptance of the fact that we who are on lower levels cannot understand every action happening on higher levels yet we are invited to witness what is happening. We are limited in our understanding. It is here that we can greatly improve. It is here that we can construct and build. This is our learning grounds. This is our Yeshiva. This is where we can grow. Mystically speaking as we are drawn to higher levels our consecration MUST proceed us. Our senses may be dull from our failure to Observe all the Mitzvot of Ha Torah. One must be careful to be sensitive to one's own soul by not consuming blood or non kosher products that darkens and clouds ones Spirituality, i.e. one's Spiritual vision.

Dear Reader, our focus now switches to the fourth point. My brothers related the following story to me decades ago.

When I was growing up at home my parents were lenient with curfew. I cannot remember ever having a curfew placed on me. Then after I left home things changed for my brothers. Gary and Roger were in their twenties. Mom and Dad, may they rest in peace, placed a 10:00PM curfew on them. I remember my brothers phoning me to complain. They wanted me to speak to Mom and Dad about lightening up. I phoned my parents. My Dad informed me that my brothers needed to get out on their own. He was keeping the 10:00 PM curfew on them until they found a place of their own. Both were working and earning excellent incomes so renting a place together was not an issue.

A few days later it seems my brothers went out on the town and tied a couple of good ones on. They returned home to find out Momma had locked the top lock. Their house keys would not work. They could not get in. And besides this my brothers looked through the front entrance door to see Momma asleep in her rocking chair just a few feet away. It was late they had been out drinking. It was snowing lightly. What were they to do?

They went to the side of the house to see if Momma had locked their bedroom window. The window was open about two inches. I think my youngest brother Roger bent down so Gary could climb up on his shoulders. They may have fell over several times... Eventually Gary managed to push the window open and fall on to his bed where he went to sleep. Roger is outside calling Gary to no avail. Roger had to jump up several feet then pull himself up to fall in the bed. When he did he fell in on Gary and made a ruckus. He quickly pulled the covers up because Momma heard. Momma poked her head in the room to see my brothers in their beds. She said something like how did you boys get in here? How did you get past me. They did not say a word. The next morning Momma quizzed them but she didn't get anywhere. Around that time I visited. We had a long prayer meeting down on our knees. It was for at least an hour. This was the way we were accustomed to praying. This was years before I began my return to Judaism. Several weeks later my brothers moved into their own apartment. What is the point? Ha Torah Says the entrance to the Tent of Meetings was open. It was not closed. No one was locked out. My brothers missed the curfew and as a result were locked out. Mamma was a guardian waiting at the entrance. They did not want to face Momma.

Those who convert to Judaism sometimes feel locked out. Those who return to Judaism sometimes feel left out. In addition some feel closely watched. When I returned to Torah Observance it seemed like the congregation of about one-hundred families that I attended had a hundred Rabbis... Everyone seemed to be watching and offering me guidance. Yet, these are feelings that the one who returns must work to overcome. We are NOT locked out!! Guidance is for our benefit. The absence of our understanding and Observing Ha Torah may cause us to think many incorrect thoughts. It is up to us to press in. It is up to us to find the path of Ha Torah and to carefully follow it. Those who convert read the Words B'nei Yisroel and wonder, how can I be from a tribe if my ancestors were not Jewish.

Well being physically from a tribe is only one consideration. Being Spiritually from a tribe is another. Many individuals who convert are connected to the Observances of Ha Torah through their Soul. Every Jewish Soul stood at Mt Sinai to Receive Ha Torah. Each of us said, We will Do and we will Hear. Going back through the Genealogies of time carries each of us to Noach and his wife, Na'amah. Were Noach and Na'amah Jewish? No! Yet, They were Very Spiritual parents. Each of us descended through them. We may not be able to see or to understand the power of this connection yet it exists. Remember Avraham had thousands of converts to Torah Observance that did not go down into Mitzriam. They believed and followed Ha Torah according to Avraham's Teachings. Do NOT be dismayed! Bereisheit Speaks to these individuals. Their root and their Observances in Judaism is deep.

Bereisheit 14.14

וַיִּשְׁמַע אַבְרָם כִּי נִשְׁבָּה אָחִיו וַיָּרֶק **אֶת־חֲנִיכָיו** יְלִידֵי בֵיתוֹ שְׁמֹנָה עָשָׂר וּשְׁלֹשׁ מֵאוֹת וַיִּרְדֹּף עַד־דָּן :

Genesis 14.14

And when Abram heard that his brother was taken captive, he armed **everything from Aleph to Tav of his trained servants,** who were born in his household, three hundred and eighteen, and pursued them to Dan.

The Words אֶת־חֲנִיכָיו Et Chah Nee Chaw mean Look these servants were trained in Yeshiva of Avraham. Rashi Says, חֲנִיכָיו is in reference to an Institute of Learning the Mitzvot of Ha Torah. Rabbi Meir Zlotowitz and Rabbi Nosson Scherman, The Artscroll Tanach Series - Bereishis Vol. I(a) (Brooklyn, New York: Mesorah Publications, Ltd. 3rd Impression, 1989), p 487 / Rabbi Nosson Scherman, The Stone Edition The Chumash (Mesorah Publications, Ltd., Brooklyn, N.Y. 1993), p 63

These Trained Servants were trained by Avraham from conception forward. Rav Elazar Said these servants were 'Torah Scholars'. In Nedarim 32a Mystically we see these Trained Servants... The Torah Scholars... These students trained in the school of Avraham as the witnesses. The Gematria of חֲנִיכָיו Chah Nee Caw is 104. This is the same Gematria of לְעֵד Lih Ahd meaning 'To Witness.'

חֲנִיכָיו
Chah Nee Caw / Trained
104 = 6ו 10י 20כ 10י 50נ 8ח

לְעֵד
Lih Ahd / To Witness
104 = 4ד 70ע 30ל

The Lord God Instructed Moshe to place Ha Torah inside the Ark of The Covenant as a witness, Deuteronomy 31.26. Why is this significant? Rav Elazar Said these 318 trained students from Avraham's Yeshiva were Torah Scholars. They also had Ha Torah within them. We Mystically see this with the Gematria 104.

No one knows what happened to these Torah

Scholars. They evaporated into thin air so to speak. They were not spoken of again. Did they follow Yitzchok? We don't know. We know the Torah Scholars did not go with Yaakov to Lavan. Genesis 32.11 informs us that Yaakov went to Lavan with nothing more than a staff. Our Sages inform us that Yaakov cried in Genesis 29.11 because he had nothing to give to Rochel where as Avraham's servant Eliezer brought camels laden with gifts for Rivkah. Why? Elifaz, the son of Eisov took everything from Yaakov. Rabbi Avrohom Davis, The Mesudah Chumash A New Linear Translation Bereishis (Hoboken New Jersey, KTVA Publishing House, Inc., 1991) p 324

When Yaakov flees Lavan He travels to 'His Brethren' in Mount Gilod as noted in Genesis 31,32; 37; 54. No one seems to know who 'His Brethren' are. Ha Torah tells us Lavan brought Kinsman with him in pursuit of Yaakov. These would be Lavan's brethren. They were not interested in Yaakov's welfare. Ask, Why would Yaakov flee if he had nothing to be afraid of? When Yaakov fled, would it seem reasonable to flee towards an area where they would be safety? Would Yaakov flee towards the witnesses? Would Yaakov flee in the direction of his Grandfather's trained Servants? Is it possible that the individuals Yaakov makes reference to as 'My Brethren' were Avraham's trained Servants? Perhaps.

Bereisheit 31.44

וְעַתָּה לְכָה נִכְרְתָה בְרִית אֲנִי וָאָתָּה וְהָיָה לְעֵד בֵּינִי וּבֵינֶךָ:

Now we know that God Spoke to the wicked Lavan. We know God Warned Lavan. Would a wicked man like Lavan pursue Yaakov in such a great display of rigger just to leave without what he came for? Ha Torah Informs us that Lavan traveled the distance of seven days in just a day, Genesis 31.23. This indicates anger and rigger. Aside from the warning from God what would make Lavan leave without what he came for? What would dissuade Lavan. It is possible Yaakov fled to his Grandfather's trained servants to His Torah Scholars and turned to them for support? I don't know.

Is it possible that in Genesis 31.24 the correct translation is *'And it happened the [Torah Scholars] witnessed between me and you...?'* It is possible, yet we don't know! We know the Gematria referring to the 'Trained' Torah Scholars in Genesis 14.14 and the witness of Genesis 31.44 is the Gematria of 104. We also know that the Word מֵאֲחֵיהֶם Mah Ah Chah Ham meaning from brethren or brothers is the Gematria of 104.

מֵאֲחֵיהֶם

Mah Ah Chah Ham / brethren or brothers

104 = 40 ם 5 ה 10 י 8 ח 1 א 40 מ

Regardless, the point is that Avraham had a Yeshiva where he trained those from children to adults. They became Torah Scholars. Then little else is spoken about them. We do not read of a connection between the Trained Servants becoming The People of Israel.

To help expand on the thought of 318 trained servants 'BORN IN HIS HOUSEHOLD' each had a father and mother and possibly brothers and sisters. In other Words there were thousands who learned in the Yeshiva of Avraham and who were a part of his household. What became of them? We don't know. Yet they had righteous Torah Observant souls. One can argue that just as they disappeared they may reappear. It is possible that these souls are manifest today in those who have this burning desire to Observe Ha Torah... It is likely that they are some of the witnesses that stood at Mount Sinai. It is also possible that many who read this book may be a descendant from one of these if they have this unquenchable thirst to be Jewish and entirely Observe Ha Torah. What and how The Lord God apportions Souls is a complete mystery. What I am trying to say is that Ha Torah is a Mystical Book and many Mystical things happen that one cannot necessarily explain.

Notice two of the Words in Verse four, אֶל־פֶּתַח Ehl - Peh Sah Ach {to the entrance}. The Tent of

Meeting here is referred to as '*the entrance to the Tent of Meeting.*' The word Peh Sah Ach to open, to throw open shares an important point. One enters into Judaism. One does NOT exit. We do not speak of an exiting. Entering into Judaism is not like changing shoes. It is like one size fits all. We all enter through the same entrance. We each are to Observe the same 613 Mitzvot of Ha Torah. No one receives special favor when it comes to Observances. We each are required to Observe the Teachings of HaTorah. It is not like trying on clothes where if one does not like the color, the style, the fit, the material or the cost they could just return the clothes. Judaism is a way of life. One enters into Judaism through birth or conversion. One does not exit. The point is that NO ONE EXITS! Messianics who are Jewish CANNOT exit Judaism or the 613 Observances of Ha Torah. They will be held accountable by The Lord God for false teachings just as any of us who do the same thing. Their children and grandchildren will suffer. Jews who do not Observe or hold Sabbath in proper regard of Holiness will be accountable!! Those of us who do this will be held accountable for our incorrect actions. We do not exit being Jewish. We each are accountable to Observe every Mitzvot placed before us!! Here in this text Aharon, the High Priest entered into a position that would only be vacant at his death. When we, The People of Israel made a commitment to our Creator we are expected to fulfill our commitment. The Lord took us as His Holy People, i.e.those born into Judaism and those who convert into Judaism. He chose us. We are separated unto God... We are separated unto Torah... We are separated unto Observances. That separation is always there. Sometimes it is not entirely to our liking. It may not be our preference. Yet we are separated. We can and sometimes do argue about our separation but it is still there. Sometimes we reject our separation but it is still there. God Has set a standard for us that we must follow. We can choose to obey what the Lord Commands us to do or we can reject His Commandments. There is no in between.

Dear Reader, there are those outside of Judaism wanting to convert that just do not know what they are getting into. They cannot understand why we Observe the Torah Portion of the Bible. They are not Jewish. The Observances are not revealed to them. Then there are those who have this burning desire that we discussed. They cannot explain why they feel the way they do but they have this drive to learn about Judaism. They are unsettled. Their Spirit is restless. It's like a huge important part of them is missing. It is likely that the Soul of these are individuals who stood at Mount Sinai to receive Ha Torah. Nothing truly fits for them. Then there are those Jews that were raised to follow other religious doctrines. They are really confused. These Jews often disagree with points in the Torah. We all fit in here somewhere. All of this is understandable. My point is to understand that Jews are required to live separated lives as defined in Ha Torah regardless of the path we are presently on! Jews are set aside unto the Lord our Creator. God Intends for Jews to live on higher levels of righteousness than other peoples of the world.

The Gematria אֶל־פֶּתַח אֹהֶל מוֹעֵד / Ehl - Peh Tah Ach Oh Hel Moh Ayd meaning to open the Tent door to the Congregation Mystically Teaches us that revelation is divided between Light and Darkness.

Bereisheit 1.4

וַיַּרְא אֱלֹהִים אֶת־הָאוֹר כִּי־טוֹב וַיַּבְדֵּל אֱלֹהִים בֵּין הָאוֹר וּבֵין הַחֹשֶׁךְ :

Genesis 1.4
And God Saw everything from Aleph to Tav of the Light [Revelation of the Torah], that it was Good; and God Divided the Light [Revelation of The Torah] from The Darkness.

בֵּין הָאוֹר וּבֵין הַחֹשֶׁךְ
Divided The Light [Revelation of the Torah] from The Darkness.
ב2 י10 ן50   ה5 א1 ו6 ר200
675 = ו6 ב2 י10 ן50   ה5 ח8 ש300 ך20

אֶל־פֶּתַח אֹהֶל מוֹעֵד
To open the Tent door to the Congregation
א1 ל30   פ80 ת400 ח8
675 = א1 ה5 ל30   מ40 ו6 ע70 ד4

The Lord's door is always open. This is the Gematria of 675. The Lord Revealed His Light, i.e. The Torah to us. I speak of אֶת־הָאוֹר / The Revelation of the Torah I discuss the revelation of Ha Torah Given to all humankind. Dr. Akiva Gamliel Belk, Mysterious Signs Of The Torah Revealed In Genesis (Cedar Hill, Missouri - B'nai Noach Torah Institute, LLC Publishers, 2012) pp 21 - 25.

The Lord Instructs us to learn Ha Torah. Then Mystically the Congregation of B'nai Yisroel sees the open Tent door to the Congregation. The Congregation realizes that a separation is taking place. The Light represented by the High Priest and the Priests is being separated from the darkness represented by B'nai Yisroel. Greater revelation is Given to Aharon the High Priest and his sons the Priests than to B'nai Yisroel. So even though our Darkness is as Light, there is a greater, more brilliant Light in the High Priest and the Priests.

Dear Ones. when our minds are clogged with misunderstandings regarding life.. regarding what

God Requires... regarding our Jewish responsibilities we are greatly constricted. Yet, if we allow ourselves to be drawn to God, by consecrating our lives then these constrictions are removed. We progress to higher levels. If we fail to return it is like being bogged down like a jeep in a vast mud hole. We cannot get out of that hole without help. We need God's Help! We cannot do it on our own. We can try but we still need God's help!

We who are on the outside of the entrance to the Tent of Meeting are on generally on lower levels of righteousness. We do not see everything. We do not understand all that we do see. We do not comprehend all that is happening on higher levels. Yet we are forced to make decisions with our limitations starring us in the face. What are we to do? There is only one way. That way is to draw into the midst of the courtyard. We are to follow behind Aharon and his sons so to speak. We are to be drawn in to the Tent of Meeting. In other words the Tent of Meeting represents greater levels of righteousness. The Tent of Meeting represents higher levels of observance.

It is in that sense we are to be drawn in.

So we see the division between us who are outside the Tabernacle and Aharon, the High Priest and his sons the Priests who are inside the Courtyard area. Our goal should be to improve!

Grading Our Holiness
Chapter Three

Parshat Shemini
Leviticus 9.1 - 11.47

Vayikra 9.1

וַיְהִי בַּיּוֹם הַשְּׁמִינִי קָרָא מֹשֶׁה לְאַהֲרֹן וּלְבָנָיו וּלְזִקְנֵי יִשְׂרָאֵל: וַיֹּאמֶר אֶל־אַהֲרֹן קַח־לְךָ עֵגֶל בֶּן־בָּקָר לְחַטָּאת וְאַיִל לְעֹלָה תְּמִימִם וְהַקְרֵב לִפְנֵי יְהוָה: וְאֶל־בְּנֵי יִשְׂרָאֵל תְּדַבֵּר לֵאמֹר קְחוּ שְׂעִיר־עִזִּים לְחַטָּאת וְעֵגֶל וָכֶבֶשׂ בְּנֵי־שָׁנָה תְּמִימִם לְעֹלָה:

Leviticus 9.1

And it came to pass on the eighth day, that Moses called Aaron and his sons, and the elders of Israel; And he said to Aaron, Take a young calf for a sin offering, and a ram for a burnt offering, without blemish, and offer them before the Lord.

We know that there are times when Jews do what is righteous, pure, Holy and correct. The same can be said for the B'nai Noach. Then there are sometimes when Jews and non-Jews walk a too close to the edge. There is a gray area where the two sides meet. In the gray area there is a thin line between being pure, Holy and correct and from being evil, sinful and wrong. In the gray area one could easily drift from one side to the other if they were not careful. This is a difficulty of living in or near the gray area. One can be shrewd in business and then quickly drift into improper business behavior. Therefore it is good to make a fence between the area we know to be pure, Holy and correct behavior from that of where the gray area begins. This way we are always careful to live in the pure, Holy and correct areas of life.

There was a sharp young businessman. He, his parents and grandparents were pillars of the Jewish Community. He and his wife had just returned from living in Israel. He returned to operate the family business so his parents could move to Israel. They owned businesses in

America and in Israel. They were successful. They have a good name. The young couple rented a house in the community. After sometime the young man and a neighbor were talking. The neighbor indicated he would like to sell his home. The young man inquired how much he wanted for his home. The price was considerably lower than its actual value. The young man made the deal. Some of us might call this an awesome business deal. Others might say he swindled the neighbor. I don't know. After the deal was made the neighbor learned what the value of his property was worth and became angry.

So we must inquire, Was the young businessman responsible for educating the neighbor on the value of property in the area? Was the neighbor careless and reckless and just looking for someone to blame. I don't know! I don't know the entire story. This may have been an issue for the Community Rav to settle or the Bet Din / Jewish Court to settle. Did this young man break any local, county, state or government laws. I am not aware of any local, county, state or government laws that were broken. Yet, I ask, 'What is so different from grabbing the best deal possible from an unlearned, poor neighbor' Wouldn't most people of the world rush down to their attorney and have a deal drawn up as quickly as possible before the neighbor learned of the true value? Unfortunately yes! So why are we discussing this? It is because, God Has His own Law that we are compelled to abide by. So the next question is did this young man break God's law?

Perhaps... We don't know the entire situation or the conversation between the parties. The matter was not brought before the Community Rav or a Jewish Bet Din.

This goes back to chapters one and two where we made a case that we are our brother's keeper and that we have a moral and ethical obligation to our brother. How far does this care and goodwill for a brother extend? To what degree are each of us responsible for our brother? We have Ha Torah, God's Law, we have Rabbinic Law and we have our own Law. This is why we Examine ourselves and grade our level of Holiness. No matter how righteous we are if we walk a little too close to the edge we could get into trouble.

Dear Reader, in Judaism we teach that one should not dress as the nations of the world. We teach that our clothes should be modest. We teach that men should wear gentlemen's apparel and that women should wear ladies' apparel. We go to great lengths to dress in a very modest fashion. We do this because we are NOT supposed to be like the other nations of the world. This is a form of building a line of modesty and keeping it. Our actions MUST correspond with our way of dressing.

As observant Jews we make so much out of the fact we changed our pattern of daily worship. We no longer prostrate ourselves before God with the exceptions of Rosh HaShanah and Yom Kippur. WHY? Why did we change our pattern of worship? It was because the nations of the world prostrate themselves in their worship. We changed because we are commanded to be different.

The point is that Jews have a higher power that we give account to and that we must ALWAYS be aware of and act accordingly!! We are supposed to be righteous! We are supposed to be honest in our business dealings. We are supposed to be above reproach! IT IS NOT GOOD TO ACT DIFFERENT IN BUSINESS THAN IN PRAYER... IT IS NOT GOOD TO DRESS THE PART OF A RIGHTEOUS JEW YET CONDUCT BUSINESS LIKE SUTAN (SATAN), God forbid!! God calls ALL JEWS to a higher level of righteousness. Unlike the nations of the world, we are chosen... we are separated... we are elected to righteousness! WE MUST LIVE LIKE IT!

Dear Reader, there are only seven days of the week however in a few places of the Torah Portion of the Bible we read about the eighth day as we do here in this Parshat of Leviticus. This has special meaning. It was on the eighth day, 1 Nisan, the Jewish new year, the beginning of months, that our Mishkon service... our Temple worship began... וַיְהִי בַּיּוֹם הַשְּׁמִינִי equals the Gematria 504. Also there is a place in this weeks Parshat that is known as the center of The Torah portion of the Bible. The halfway point between the first half of the Torah and the second half of the Torah is marked by the words דָּרֹשׁ דָּרַשׁ Daw Rahsh Daw Rahsh meaning to diligently inquire makes the center word of the Torah Inquiry! This is what our discussion is about. We are to diligently inquire about our actions.

וַיְהִי בַּיּוֹם הַשְּׁמִינִי
And On the Eighth Day...
וּ6 יִ10 הַ5 יִ10   בַּ2 יִ10 וּ6 מִ40
504 = הַ5 שׁ300 מִ40 יִ10 נִ50 יִ10

דָּרֹשׁ
Daw Rahsh
To Diligently Inquire
504 = דּ4 ר200 שׁ300

Vayikra 10.16 [The Center of Ha Torah]

וְאֵת | שְׂעִיר הַחַטָּאת דָּרֹשׁ דָּרַשׁ מֹשֶׁה וְהִנֵּה
שֹׂרָף וַיִּקְצֹף עַל־אֶלְעָזָר וְעַל־אִיתָמָר
בְּנֵי אַהֲרֹן הַנּוֹתָרִם לֵאמֹר:

Leviticus 10.16
And Moses **diligently sought** the goat of the

sin offering, and, behold, it was burned; and he was angry with Eleazar and Ithamar, the sons of Aaron, who were left alive, saying,

Few of us are anywhere near the level of the righteousness of Aharon's two sons who crossed the line a little. Crossing the line is serious, especially for a very righteous person, is quite serious. Yet we know,

Psalm 37.12,24
The steps of a good man are ordered by the Lord: and He delights in his way. Though he fall, he shall not be utterly cast down: for the Lord Will uphold him with his hand.

As noted above many translate 'The steps of a good man are ordered by the Lord:' However the correct translation is The Steps of the Strong are Ordered by The Lord and He Delights in His Way.

Judging and correcting one actions takes great strength. One must be just with their self. One must not be to strict or to lenient. This is a fine line to walk.

This is why we inquire about our actions.

Many years ago while sitting in a packed auditorium as a Junior High student at Morey Middle School in Denver, Colorado, I heard Principle George E. Mathes relate the following story. Principle Mathes said, *There was a little boy named Billie who was about twelve years. Billie worked for the local drugstore as a delivery boy. He would ride all over town on his shiny red bike with chrome fenders.*

One day Billie came into the local Ice Cream store which was located a block or so down the street from the drug store where he worked. He climbed up on the stool, sat down and ordered a ice cream shake. After ordering the ice cream shake he asked the owner, Mr. Fisher if it would be alright for him to use his phone for a local call. Mr. Fisher said, Sure. Billie went to the end of the counter and made his call. Mr. Fisher over heard the following conversation.

Billie said, Hello, could I speak with the owner of Smith's Drug Store.

Mr. Smith answered, Yes! This is Mr Smith.

Billie inquired, Mr. Smith, I hear you are looking for a delivery boy.

*Mr. Smith said, No! We have a delivery boy.
Billie said, I hear he is not doing a good job. Are you sure you don't need a new delivery boy.*

Mr Smith said, Our delivery boy is Billie Jones. He is johnny on the spot. He is polite to our customers. He is quick to make his deliveries. We are very pleased with him. You must be thinking about another delivery boy somewhere else.

Billie hung the phone up. His Ice Cream Shake was just about ready. As Billie sat there enjoying his Ice Cream Soda. Mr Fisher asked Billie a question.

Billie I thought you were the delivery boy for Mr.

Smith's Drug Store down on the corner.

Billie said, I am.

Mr Fisher asked, Can I ask why you called to see if Mr. Smith needed a delivery boy?

Billie said, Yes! I was just checking up on myself. I want to make sure Mr. Smith is pleased with my delivery service.

This is the type of attitude I am trying to draw out in this discussion. We need to check on ourselves. We also need to remember that when a strong man or woman fails the Lord Will help them back up again.

In this week's Parshat, the Midrash states that our Sages determined that there are three methods to evaluate an individual's character. This discussion results because of Moshe our Teacher's momentary anger and the unfortunate deaths of Nodov and Avihu, Aharon's sons who were intoxicated when they offered 'strange fire' before The Lord. They died because of their sin!

Our Sages identify the three areas of character evaluation as:

Bekoso: Observe one's drinking habits. Excessive drinking results in loose language and displays a lack of self restraint. One who controls his liquor is in control of himself / herself!

Bekiso: Observe ones business habits. Our Sages Teach that a person's way of conducting business is revealing of one's attitude toward his fellow man. By observing if one acts righteously... honestly... fairly towards his fellow man or by observing if one seeks to shortchange his fellow man we can measure his relationship to his fellow man!

Beka'aso: Observe one's temper. Anyone who loses his temper in a fit of rage, who throws things, tears clothing or damages things is considered like an idol worshiper by our Sages. If he allows his / her evil inclination to dominate to that extent, then that one is capable of idol worship, God forbid. Rabbi Moshe Weissman, The Midrash Says (Brooklyn, New York: Benei

Now, Dear Reader, it is so important how we conduct ourselves. If we dress black and white and look like Orthodox Jews then we are expected to live on that level. Still, regardless of how we dress we must be careful to manage our liquor... our business dealings... our temper... Parshat Shemini is a challenge to each of us! It was on the eighth day, 1 Nisan, the Jewish new year, the beginning of months, that our Mishkon service... our Temple worship began. With our newly constructed Mishkon in the wilderness we are challenged to improve, to confess our sin, to bring offerings and to live on a much higher level than in the past. The same is true for us today. We are to clean and dedicate the Spiritual Mishkon within each of us. We are to elevate our lives with holiness.

Change the World with ONE Action
Chapter Four

Parshat Tazria
Leviticus 12.1 -13.59

Vayikra 13.13

וְרָאָה הַכֹּהֵן וְהִנֵּה כִסְּתָה הַצָּרַעַת אֶת־כָּל־בְּשָׂרוֹ וְטִהַר אֶת־הַנָּגַע כֻּלּוֹ הָפַךְ לָבָן **טָהוֹר** הוּא:

Leviticus 13.13
Then the priest shall consider; and, behold, if the leprosy has covered everything from Aleph to Tav of all his flesh, he shall pronounce him everything from Aleph to Tav clean, he who has the disease; it is all turned white; he is clean.

There are individuals with sin rooted deep within them. Then there are individuals like this poor leper with all his sin exposed for the entire world to see. His sin is obvious to all who come in contact with him. His error remains for a short while then new skin is generated by his body replaces the old white skin with leprosy. He is clean. He is טָהוֹר הוּא. He / She returns to the Jewish Community as a changed man / woman.

Vayikra 13.35, 36

וְאִם־פָּשֹׂה יִפְשֶׂה הַנֶּתֶק בָּעוֹר אַחֲרֵי טָהֳרָתוֹ: וְרָאָהוּ הַכֹּהֵן וְהִנֵּה פָּשָׂה הַנֶּתֶק בָּעוֹר לֹא־יְבַקֵּר הַכֹּהֵן לַשֵּׂעָר הַצָּהֹב טָמֵא הוּא:

Leviticus 13.35,36

And if the patch did spread much over the skin after his cleansing; Then the priest shall look on him; and, behold, if the patch has spread over the skin, the priest shall not seek for yellow hair; he is **unclean**.

This is an individual who sin is deeper than the surface of the skin. Originally He / She was declared clean because the leprosy appeared to be just on the surface. Later it becomes clear that the leprosy is deeper rooted than the surface.

In Parshat Tazria there are two unique words each of which begins with the same letter, the letter ט Tet. The words are Taw Hoor {clean} and Taw May {not clean}.

טָהוֹר
Taw Hoor {clean}
220 = 200ר 6ו 5ה 9ט

Taw May {not clean}
50 = 1א 40מ 9ט

What did The Spirit of God do when Moving upon the void unformed desolate and dark waters in Genesis 1.2?

וְרוּחַ
Vih Ruach
And Spirit [moved]
220 = 8ח 6ו 200ר 6ו

Mystically the Spirit purges and cleanses.

The letter ט Tet represents 'goodness' seeing as the letter ט Tet is the first letter of the word Tov meaning 'Good'. Then I mentioned that the Letter ט Tet was deliberately left out of the First

Tablets Of Stone given to Moshe on Har Sinai because if they had contained the letter ט Tet which represents 'Good', then when Moshe smashed the Tablets into pieces it would have been a sign that all goodness had come to an end on the earth.

Now, Dear holy readers, the exact opposite is also true. In a world encompassed by evil the Letter ט Tet can bring forth goodness. Just as social workers use terms like the cycle of abuse... the cycle of hate... the cycle of grief ... the cycle of evil... Our Sages tell the story of an evil king who did one good deed in his entire lifetime and thus beginning the a cycle of good. The Lord Blessed that evil king's action. Eglon, king of Moav who was a sinfully wicked king, received a messenger named Ehud. The Tenach states:

Judges 3.20
Ehud came to him [King Eglon who was very obese] *while he was sitting alone in his cool upper chamber. Ehud said, 'I have a Word of God for you,'* [King Eglon] *stood up from his*

chair, [even though standing was extremely difficult for him].

This may seem insignificant until you know the rest of the story. Our rabbium state that anyone who recites Kaddish should stand. Why? If this extremely wicked king of Moav stood to receive a Word from God we should do likewise. As a result this wicked king has altered the world. Now millions of Yidden stand for Kaddish because of his single solitary action. Dear Reader, in a similar way we can change the world. One action can give light... Thomas Edison. One action can give instant communication... Alexander Graham Bell. One action can change the world. We see this in the Gematria Permutation of Taw May.

Gematria Permutation
Taw May {not clean}
Aleph = 1 Mem = 40 Tet = 9   **360 =** 9 x 40 x 1

So we can see within the word Taw May is the Gematria Permutation of 360. We know that 360 degrees represents a complete circle.... a full cycle... a complete cycle. Unfortunately that circle or cycle is derived from the word Taw May meaning unclean. It is as if to say the entire world is unclean. It is as if to say the entire world is filled with a cycle of uncleanness. On an individual level it is as if to say, 'How can I break the cycle of violence... abuse... drugs...?'

A number of years ago I took a break from business around lunchtime to take care of some errands. Sometimes while running errands I included two very special little friends, my year and a half old twin beagles, Kalie and Dov. They provided so much company! As we were returning from an errand, Dovie looked up at me with those big brown, sad eyes, as if to say, *'Could we please go for a run? Please!'* We were close to an area they particularly loved to run in. Any time we are close to that area, they begin whimpering. I know what they want!

We went to this area where they occasionally run. Normally I let them out of the vehicle on a seldom used dirt road and they follow behind for aways. Howeverrrrrrrrrrrrrrrrrrrrr, on this occasion,

Kalie picked up the scent of bighorn sheep and instead of running behind the vehicle he immediately turned to the left and began climbing this steep, rocky mountain like a billy goat. It was absolutely phenomenal watching him go over rocks much larger than him, like a caterpillar with plungers on his feet. Up and down and around and over the rocks he went with his heavy little brother behind him. I stopped the vehicle, set the emergency break and jumped out, beckoning him to stop and to return to me. It was as if Kalie was in a trance. Nothing I said made any difference! He was so concentrated and focused on following that scent that my words couldn't reach him. Nose to the ground, tail waving in the air... then came the bellows, every third or fourth step, as only a beagle can do. I knew he was gone and it seemed as if there was nothing I could do.

Both he and his brother were climbing farther and farther up the mountain. I called to his brother, 'Dov! Come Tatty!' Dov stopped. He turned to look at me. I gave him a loving motion to come back to me. He did. With that one action, he chose me over his twin brother, over his powerful instinct to hunt and over his desire to have fun. He came down the mountainside right to me. And there is no way I can tell you how proud I was! We went to the vehicle, he got in, poked his head out the window, and began calling his brother. These boys love each other very much. About ten years later when my former spouse chose a different direction in life she took these little boys. I could have fought for one but how could I separate these two brothers? They were now older guys. They had been together since being in the womb. Back to the story - It is very difficult for them when they are separated. Kalie was near the top of the mountain. Dov was in the truck with me. Kalie climbed over a thousand feet up the mountain side. He was out of my voice range and almost out of my sight. Dov began to howl and cry. He heard his brother beckoning in that high pitched sound of his. He halted in his footsteps and immediately began his return to us.

Dear Reader, this is an example of how one very positive, dedicated action can alter a situation. Had Dov not returned to me, the hunt, the following of the scent could have lasted for days. And certainly hours. In the same way, we can use our influence with those we influence and they will influence others. One act can change the world.

That days the boys took off up the mountainside, Interstate 70 was a few hundred feet away. The truck was parked on the dirt road and the mountain high mountain was next to it. When the boys took off I immediately had visions of them chasing wildlife which is against the law and of them trying to cross this huge interstate with a four foot divider between east and west lanes. I was very worried this may be the last time I would see them alive. I cried out to the Lord. He Heard my desperate cry and somehow brought those two little beagle boys back to me.

When one has only one Word from the Torah with three letters that spell טָמֵא 'unclean' it may seem like there is little hope. Don't give up. The Letter Tet represents Goodness. The Letter Mem represents Mysteries and Mysticism. The Letter Aleph represents God. Even though the present position of these Letters spells 'Unclean' there is another side that spells hope. Don't give up. Explore. Gematria is about exploring. Change the Letters around.

טָמֵא
Taw Mahy / Uncleanness

מאט
Retardant

אטם
To Close, To Shut Off, To Seal

Gematria Ragil
טָמֵא
50 = 1א 40מ 9ט

Gematria Miluy Mispar Katan
טָמֵא
14= 1א 4מ 9ט

Gematria Miluy
ט = טית = 419
419 = 400ת 10י 9ט

מ = מם = 80
מ40 כ40 = 80

א = אלף= 111
א1 ל30 ף80 = 111

610 = 419 + 80 + 111
Gematria Miluy Godal
Final Letters
ט = טית = 419
ט9 י10 ת40 = 419

מ = מם = 80
מ40 כ600 = 640

א = אלף= 111
א1 ל30 ף800 = 831

1890 = 419 + 640 + 831

When it seems like there is no place to turn we just explore… STUDY the possibilities. Remember that for every Yes Gematria there is a no Gematria. For every left Gematria there is a right Gematria.

Now this is how we change the world with only one action. We alter Taw May. We change the Letters around. We study the Gematria numbers, Letters. We don't change the Goodness represented by the Tet. We can't change our Creator represented by the Aleph. We cannot change the mystery represented by the Mem. One should also note that the final letter Mem represents a 360 degree circle. It is a mysterious circle.

There are three Letters that we can rearrange and there are at least four numbers we study the Gematria of. There are many relationships to the four numbers if we take the time to learn them. Some may not be revealed to us. Then we have the option of exchanging the Letter א Aleph for the Letter ע Ayin. The point is that when one is in a difficult place there is hope. There are options. We may not see them but just the same they are there. A portion of Mysticism is how do we see and understand the Mystical revelations in our realm.

For example, uncleanness often comes from

touching a dead body, or animal. Uncleanness comes from touching a lady who is unclean from her time of the month... Yet purification comes from the earth we were taken from. Our last form of purification is when we return to the earth and our body decays in the אֲדָמָה / earth.

אֲדָמָה
Earth
50 = 5ה 40מ 4ד 1א

From this we can see that our final repentance will be through the decay of our unclean body in the the earth. The number fifty is associated with the fifty levels of righteousness. It about the direction we choose.

מַיִם
Water
50 = 10י 40מ

It is interesting to note that the first two letters of water is the Gematria 50. Water is always plural. We really cannot define just a drop of water. A drop is always more than a drop. What is the point. Gematria can also point us in the direction we need to go even if it is not complete...

כָּל
Kawl
All, Whole, Complete..
50 = 30ל 20כ
What does it mean to be Mystically whole or complete?

Dear Reader, we can break the cycle of uncleanness by simply changing one action. One action changes the essence of Taw May to many possible words and numbers. Every Gematria is important and powerful.

Sanctifying An Unclean House At Passover
Chapter Five

Parshat Metzoro
Leviticus 14.1 – 15.33

Vayikra 14.43

וְאִם־יָשׁוּב **הַנֶּגַע** וּפָרַח בַּבַּיִת אַחַר חִלֵּץ אֶת־הָאֲבָנִים וְאַחֲרֵי הִקְצוֹת אֶת־הַבַּיִת וְאַחֲרֵי הִטּוֹחַ: וּבָא הַכֹּהֵן וְרָאָה וְהִנֵּה פָּשָׂה הַנֶּגַע בַּבָּיִת צָרַעַת מַמְאֶרֶת הִוא בַּבַּיִת טָמֵא הוּא: וְנָתַץ אֶת־הַבַּיִת אֶת־אֲבָנָיו וְאֶת־עֵצָיו וְאֵת כָּל־עֲפַר הַבָּיִת וְהוֹצִיא אֶל־מִחוּץ לָעִיר אֶל־מָקוֹם טָמֵא:

Leviticus 14.43

*And if **the disease** comes again, and break out in the house, after he has taken away the stones, and after he has scraped the house, and after it is plastered; Then the priest shall come and look, and, behold, if the disease has spread in the house, it is a malignant leprosy in the house; it is unclean. And he shall break down the house,* *its stones, and its timber, and all the mortar of the house; and he shall carry them out of the city into an unclean place.*

A while back, in a separate discussion not in this book, in Shemot Shemot we discussed Shuvah / Repentance. At that time I stated many of the world's population were preparing to turn over a new leaf. Then a few weeks later while studying in Parshat Beshalach I stated, 'We have entered our fourth week from Parshat Shemot / January 2000.' Already many who made a determination to alter their poor or improper actions, to do shuvah / repentance to be free from habits... from bondage... and from problems have fallen. During the past three weeks we discussed the monsters that bring us down, that help us fall and that help us to fail.'

Well, Dear Reader, we are now 13 plus years from that date where many made a determination to change. That being the situation, we must assess where we aret. Have we returned to the bondage we so desperately attempted to escape from? Have old habits / addictions crept back?

Have we fallen?

If the answer is perhaps or yes please do not become discouraged. **There is HOPE!!** There is a Spiritual Season for Freedom. There is a festival for freedom, a special time that The Lord God Created for us to deal with those issues that have bound us. It is during this time frame that we can deal with everything about our nature, our shortcomings, our failures and our struggles more than we could ever. imagine.   This is one reason why The Lord stated in Parshat Metzozo

Vayikra 14.35, 26

וּבָא אֲשֶׁר־לוֹ הַבַּיִת וְהִגִּיד לַכֹּהֵן לֵאמֹר **כְּנֶגַע** נִרְאָה לִי בַּבָּיִת: וְצִוָּה הַכֹּהֵן וּפִנּוּ אֶת־הַבַּיִת בְּטֶרֶם יָבֹא הַכֹּהֵן לִרְאוֹת **אֶת־הַנֶּגַע** וְלֹא יִטְמָא כָּל־אֲשֶׁר בַּבָּיִת וְאַחַר כֵּן יָבֹא הַכֹּהֵן לִרְאוֹת אֶת־הַבָּיִת:

Leviticus 14.35 - 45

And he who owns the house shall come to the priest, tell him, saying, **It seems like** *there is a disease in the house. Then the priest shall command that they empty everything from Aleph to Tav of the house*

before the priest shall go in to see **everything from Aleph to Tav of the disease,** *so that all that is in the house not be made unclean; and afterwards the priest shall go in to see everything from Aleph to Tav of the house.*

Notice the Words אֶת־הַנֶּגַע Eht Ha Naw Gah meaning everything from Aleph to Tav of the disease. There are several connections that we must make here.

First, The owner of the house calls the Kohein / The Priest. Why does the owner call The Priest? It is because נֶגַע Naw Gah, i.e. this disease is not a medical issue. נֶגַע Naw Gah is a Spiritual issue. Dear reader many of the problems that we have are spiritual in nature. These issues must be brought before The Lord God. Our Sages Teach we are discussing a disease that results from speaking Loshon Hora, i.e speaking evil... gossiping...

Second, the owner of the house must go to the Priest. The owner must take the initiative for help.

The one who owns the house has the problem. The one who has the problem must come to the realization that he / she has the problem and seek the assistance of the Priest. Note Ha Torah Does NOT Say a Rabbi. The Priest is set aside. The Priest is anointed. The Priest has a special High Level of Holiness. This is not a slam against Rabbi's. This is simply explaining why one must go to a Priest. Aharon was the High Priest as well as a Rabbi!

Third the owner who has this problem must express to The Priest that he has a potential problem and request help from The Priest.

Fourth The Priest becomes involved. The Priest has everything not attached to the house removed. The items are carried outside for all the neighbors to see. This now becomes an embarrassing humbling acknowledgement for the owner to his / her neighbors that he / she has a problem. This is an opportunity for all neighbors to come together to be loving, kind, understanding and to reach out to their fallen brother / sister and to offer to help. This is NOT a time to judge!! This is a time to be compassionate! This is a time to restore if one has fallen. Now I say 'IF' because this is not certain. The Word used in Ha Torah is כְּנֶגַע Kih Neg Gah meaning 'Like a disease'. The determination has not yet been made. This only appears like a disease. So all the Jewish Community MUST be very careful NOT to judge during this examination or after even if this is found to be a disease!!

Fifth after all items in the house have been removed The Priest enters the house to examine, אֶת־הַנֶּגַע *'...the priest shall go in to see everything from Aleph to Tav of the disease...'*

The Gematria for אֶת־הַנֶּגַע is 529. Mystically we are Informed that the purpose of the Priest's examination, For The Priest הַיְדַעְתֶּם Hah Yih Dah Tehm to know without any doubt that this is נֶגַע. The Gematria for הַיְדַעְתֶּם Hah Yih Dah Tehm. is 529.

אֶת־הַנֶּגַע
Eht Ha Neg Gah
'...*Everything from Aleph to Tav of the disease...*'
529 = 70ע 3ג 50נ 5ה   400ת 1א

הַיְדַעְתֶּם
Hah Yih Dah Tehm
The Knowledge
529 = 40ם 400ת 70ע 4ד 10י 5ה

Sixth, The Priest, i.e. a Righteous man... a Spiritual man... He examines the possible issue. He must ascertain what the issue is. This is NOT left up to conjecture! This is NOT open to speculation. He will know!!

Seventh, He will offer the guidelines for treating the issue. Much of this is done in the view of the community. This is painful! It is shameful! It is now easy for the one desiring freedom. Yet this is the path for this specific remedy. The path for each remedy must be completely followed.

Now we consider just the Neh Gah. The

Gematria of Neh Gah is 123. Let's examine 123.

נֶגַע
The **Neh Gah**
123 = 70ע 3ג 50נ

How can we be freed from this Neh Gah tzora'as? We have tried to break away from our problems, our habits, our addictions, our sins, but they have returned. Our problem is like 'THE PLAGUE' which is exactly what Hah Neh Gah is, it is 'THE PLAGUE.' Each of us have our own specially prepared pack of difficulties designed to try and to test us. However none of our errors our tests or our trials are intended to dismantle our Spiritual house. Yet, this maybe necessary if we do not heed the Observances of Ha Torah! In our discussion we are not discussing the stage of dismantling the house. Why? Because it is my sincere desire that our discussion prevent our issues from advancing to that stage. I am prayerfully hopeful that we will accept where we are and begin reversing our improper actions immediately with Spiritual assistance from Ha Torah in lieu of The priest. Remember ONLY Ha

Torah has the power to restore...

Psalm 19.8 - (KJV 19.7)
The Torah of the Lord is Perfect, Restoring the Soul; the Testimony of the Lord is sure, making wise the simple.

Dear Reader when one i.e., either from among the People of Israel or the People of Noach Observes The Commands of Ha Torah that one will be RESTORED!!

When we realize this and accept this, The Mitzvot / Commands of the first five Books of the Bible, i.e. The Torah become our spiritual program to growth, NOT DEFEATE!!

I am sharing about the opportunity to free ourselves of our issues. It is very important for us to seize this opportunity to achieve the freedom we desire and have toiled and struggled for.

We enter the realm of 123 during Passover. Pesach / Passover is the season for housecleaning both spiritual and physical. It is not the season for dismantling our house. It is the season to experience freedom. **When we enter the Passover season we enter the Creator's natural season especially designed for our freedom.** This is why the title to this chapter says, Sanctifying An Unclean House At Passover. Our yetzer Tov / Good inclination is strong. Our yetzer Tov is invigorated. Our challenger, the yetzer raw / evil inclination, is weak during this period. This is the Festival of Freedom. It is time to try with all our Yetzer Tov to succeed! It is Hah Paw Sahach / meaning 'the opening / the entrance', the Lee Zi Noohs [open] door for those of us who have been defeated time and again to return to enter freedom through.

Vayikra 14.3

וְיָצָא הַכֹּהֵן אֶל־מִחוּץ לַמַּחֲנֶה וְרָאָה הַכֹּהֵן וְהִנֵּה נִרְפָּא נֶגַע־הַצָּרַעַת מִן־הַצָּרוּעַ:

Leviticus 14.3

And the priest shall go out of the camp; and the priest shall look, and, behold, if the disease of leprosy is healed in the leper...

We are considering the Gematria of just Neh Gah in Leviticus 14.3 where the Kohen examines the individual to see if the Neg Gah tzora'as has healed so that the individual may undergo purification, where we Mystically see an interesting bond. The Gematria of Neh Gah is 123. In years where we observe the second month of Adar, the total days **from the beginning of Parshat Shemot from the first day, until the seventh day of Pesach totals 123 days.**

Let's take the year 5773 as an example:
Parshat Shemot Study began on Sunday December 30, 2012, i.e. 17 Tevet. From this point we count the days going forward to Pesach.

Tevet 13 days
Shevat 30 days
Adar (1) 29 days
Adar (2) 29 days – This year is not a leap year.
Nissan 22 days – Seventh Day of Pesach

Total   123 days

Dear Reader, even though this year is not a leap year, still from the above example one can understand how we arrive at 123 days. The point is Pesach Season is 123 days. This is the season of freedom!!

The next day which is the eighth day of Pesach is like the eighth day when the individual brings his sin offering to The Lord and the Kohen atones for him and declares him purified. This is also like the 122 / 123 days from the sin of the golden calf leading up to the Day of Atonement, Yom Kippur. These are the Seasons of Freedom.

After receiving our Freedom we must be vigilant to keep our freedom...

Vayikra 14.43

וְאִם־יָשׁוּב הַנֶּגַע וּפָרַח בַּבַּיִת מָקוֹם טָמֵא:

Leviticus 14.43
And if the ***disease*** *comes again, and breaks out in the house...*

In Leviticus 14.43 we read '...if {Hah} Neh Gah

returns'. This in reference to one's disease infested house returning after being cleansed / sanctified. This is a caution a warning about maintaining ones Sanctification... One's Holiness. One's purity... to the Lord God. We MUST be as careful as possible to NOT allow any opening to our freedoms The Lord God Provides us with! We are reminded that if we are not careful our problems can return. We do not want this so to avoid problems returning we involve ourselves in Torah Observances and Derek Ha Torah, i.e. We stay on the Path of Ha Torah.

Mystically we Observe the Gematria of 493 warning us to remain true to The Lord God, Don't permit any openings...!

וְאִם־יָשׁוּב הַנֶּגַע
Vih Eem Yaw Shoov Ha Neh Gah Aw
And if the disease return
493 = 70ע 3ג 50נ 5ה 2ב 6ו 300ש 10י 40ם 1א 6ו

לִזְנוֹת
Lee Zih Nooht / Unfaithfulness To The Lord God
493 = 400ת 6ו 50נ 7ז 30ל

הַפֶּתַח
Hah Paw Tahach / Opening - Entrance
493 = 8ח 400ת 80פ 5ה

My hope and prayer is for each of us to use the Seasons of Freedom to free ourselves of issues and to better serve our Creator by Observing His Commands.

Guarding Against Sin
Chapter 6

Parshat Acharei Mot
Leviticus 16.1 - 18.30

Vayikra 18.30

וּשְׁמַרְתֶּם אֶת־מִשְׁמַרְתִּי לְבִלְתִּי עֲשׂוֹת מֵחֻקּוֹת הַתּוֹעֵבֹת אֲשֶׁר נַעֲשׂוּ לִפְנֵיכֶם **וְלֹא תִטַּמְּאוּ בָּהֶם** אֲנִי יְהֹוָה אֱלֹהֵיכֶם׃

Leviticus 18.30
And You shall guard everything from Aleph to Tav of My Charge to you, to not do any of these abominable customs, which were committed before you, **and do not become defiled through them;** *I am The Lord your God.*

In the previous Chapter we concluded with a caution to stay on the Path of Ha Torah. Staying on the Path of Ha Torah can be a challenge.
For example: It easy to become angry and say

and do the wrong things. It is easy to let one's mind, thoughts eyes stray from the path of Ha Torah... How do we face these challenges? Facing challenges is not new to our people. In the past we have been surrounded by abominations intended to attract us to sinfulness like when The People of Israel were surrounded by abominations while living in the BaMidbar / Wilderness. There were nations intent on drawing us into there abominable customs. We had to draw together like eaglets drawn to the protection of their mother and covered by her wings. The sin that was all around us could not be permitted in Eretz Canaan. The People of Israel had to separate from these iniquities. The People of Israel had to live by a higher standard.

People who have not taken the time to carefully study The First Five Books of The Bible and who may not understand or know anything about The 613 Mitzvot / Commands from The Lord God written in The First Five Books of The Bible may take the position that the 613 Observances of Ha Torah are done away with. Many have been indoctrinated from conception to beliefs taught by their parents, their parents customs, traditions, religions just as we who Observe Ha Torah are supposed to do with our children. They believe they are correct. We believe we are correct. Many of them are zealous just as many of us are zealous. **Only The Lord God knows the Truth!** Only the Lord God Knows how we will each come together in peace at some point in the future. I am saying that today as it was in the days of Moshe people who have been raised differently than us. They have different understandings of The Lord God than we have. Some try to persuade us to act like them, believe them etc. **We MUST have a great deal of resolve to be understanding with them and to show kindness. Still we must remain committed to the Observances of Ha Torah.** Dear Reader, lets think about this. We are supposed to be the Holy People. We are supposed to be the example. This means we CANNOT act as they do. Our actions must follow the Path of Ha Torah. If they curse at us we MUST follow the Path of Ha Torah. If they are mean to us we MUST follow Ha Torah. If they try to entice us we MUST follow the Path of Ha

Torah. We MUST NOT ACT LIKE THEM!!

Just as The Lord God charged The People of Israel then, we are charged now! The Lord God Said,

Leviticus 18.30
And You [The People of Israel] shall guard everything from Aleph to Tav of My Charge to you, to not do any of these abominable customs, which were committed before you, **and do not become defiled through them;** *I am The Lord your God.*

Now we are back to the question, How are we to do this? Well, simply put, we stand guard over our lives, over our family, over our neighbor, over our house, over our block, over our community, over our city and over our nation...

The point is that we are our keeper and we are our brother's keeper.

When I was single my next door neighbor's were the Kohn's. I lived in the basement of the house next door. They were very very special neighbors. They were like parents to me. Rabbi Kohn was always checking on me. If I did not daven / pray as part of the morning minyan at our congregation the Rabbi would ask me the next time we met where I davened that morning. A Minyan is group of ten Jewish men above the age of twelve. When one davens they pray.

On Sabbath, I would hear this tapping on my basement window. It was my neighbor, Rabbi Kohn. I could hear him saying, 'Akiva! Akiva! It's time to walk to shul for morning prayers.' He wanted to make sure I was up and about. He wanted to make sure I was going to be at the congregation for morning prayers.

On one Erev Sabbath he was on his way to services. I just pulled up to my apartment in my old brown truck. He was going to wait for me to get ready so we could walk to congregation together. I said, I need to go to the store quickly.

He said, 'What for?'
I said, 'I need a few things?'

Rabbi Kohn said, 'What do you need? It is almost time for Sabbath to begin?'

I said, 'A few groceries and some whiskey.

Rabbi Khon was a short man but that did not get in his way. He reached up to me with both hands and firmly took hold of my lapels and pulled me down right in front of his face and firmly but kindly said, 'Akiva listen to me! You come eat a my house this Sabbath. You drink all the whiskey you want at my house. Now, park your truck. Empty your pockets. Let's walk together. It's time to Observe Sabbath.'

What could I say? I did as instructed. I ate all three meals with the Kohn's. It was real special. That Sabbath Rabbi Kohn invited a guest to come dine with us after Evening Prayers. He invited a Chassidic Rabbi from Israel, may he rest in peace. Dear Ones, we MUST care about each other. We must be like the soldiers whose motto is not to leave anyone behind. Then in addition to us caring about our own we MUST show gentle loving care and be kind to all humans, i.e. the Noachide.

The Lord Chose us, the Jewish people, as His people. The Lord Chooses Eretz Yisroel as the earthly location for His Dwelling place, the Bet HaMikdosh, the Holy Temple. When I say Holy I am saying 'SEPARATED'. The OBSERVANCES of The Mitzvot of Ha Torah Make The People of Israel Holy, Make the Temple Holy, Make the City of Jerusalem Holy, Make the Land of Yisroel Holy. Our Creator Say's They are Holy. Our Creator Gave us guidelines to make sure this Holiness remains. The Lord God Has Selected each of these to be Holy yet it is our duty as the Jewish People to keep these important Observances. We are the ones who follow the directives that separate The Holy Things. Holiness is separation. Holiness is a division that is accomplished by observing Ha Torah. We, The People of Yisroel must be careful to guard all of our Torah Observances. When we do this we are guarding our Holiness. As noted earlier this is accomplished through Torah Observance. For non Jews this is accomplished through observance of the Seven Commands.

The formula for Holiness given by The Lord God to the People of Israel for Eretz Yisroel CAN ONLY BE FULFILLED BY JEWS LIVING IN ERETZ YISROEL! Even if non Jews lived in Eretz Yisroel and strictly observed The Torah Commands this would NOT FULFILL the basic requirements of making Eretz Yisroel a 'HOLY LAND' or of 'SEPARATING ERETZ YISROEL' unto The Lord! Non Jews cannot serve in or around the Bet HaMikdosh, / The Holy Temple no matter how Holy they are! Non Jews cannot be a Levi or a Kohen! In fact Jews born into a family that is not a Levi or Kohen cannot serve in or around the Bet Ha Mikdosh either, no matter how Holy they are! Speaking of the 613 Mitzvot of Ha Torah I teach a class online entitled The 613 Mitzvot of Ha Torah. It is a Free course. A number of individuals have signed up to learn one Observance from The 613 Observances of Ha Torah Each week.

WHY is this important?
The Lord God Set a standard between The People of Israel and the other nations and beliefs of the world. The Lord God Set a standard

between The People of Israel and the Levium. The Lord God Set a standard between the Levium and the Kohenim! Each standard requires a greater degree of separation, Holiness. The standard begins with being born Jewish and continues from this point onward. This standard cannot be achieved through any other means. No amount of learning or number of degrees will achieve the standard set down in the Torah by The Lord God! No amount of Holiness will achieve that standard set down by The Lord God in Ha Torah!

Some religions teach the Observances written in Ha Torah, i.e. the standards set by The Lord God have been discarded. Some teach that they have been eliminated. Some teach they have been superseded. It is for these very reasons and others that The Lord God Said to The People of Yisroel:

Vayikra 18.30

וּשְׁמַרְתֶּם אֶת־מִשְׁמַרְתִּי לְבִלְתִּי עֲשׂוֹת
מֵחֻקּוֹת הַתּוֹעֵבֹת אֲשֶׁר נַעֲשׂוּ לִפְנֵיכֶם
וְלֹא תִטַּמְּאוּ בָּהֶם אֲנִי יְהוָה אֱלֹהֵיכֶם׃

Leviticus 18.30

And You shall guard everything from Aleph to Tav of My Charge to you, to not do any of these abominable customs, which were committed before you, and do not become defiled through them; I am The Lord your God.

This is why we we, The People of Yisroel REJECT ANY NOTION THAT HA TORAH IS FULFILLED, THAT THE TORAH IS COMPLETED, THAT THE TORAH IS SUPERSEDED! It is our responsibility to guard every Observance of Ha Torah with all that we have! The Gematria for וְלֹא תִטַּמְּאוּ בָּהֶם Vih Loh Tee Tah Mihoo Baw Hehm, meaning *'and you shall not defile yourselves through them'* {any of the abominable customs...}, is 540.

וְלֹא תִטַּמְּאוּ בָּהֶם
Vih Loh Tee Tah Mihoo Baw Hehm
'and you shall not defile yourselves through them'
540 = 40מ 5ה 2ב 6ו 1א 40מ 9ט 400ת 1א 30ל 6ו

שָׁמֹר
Shaw Mohr /Guard / Keep / Observe
540 = 200ר 40מ 300ש

One is permitted to add the Letter Aleph to any Gematria because our Creator is One. The Letter aleph equals One. So if we were to add the Letter Aleph to שָׁמֹר the Gematria would be 541. This is significant because the Gematria for Israel is 541.

יִשְׂרָאל
Israel
541 = 30ל 1א 200ר 300ש 10י

Mystically we Observe that it is us, The People of יִשְׂרָאל that are to guard the Observances of Ha Torah.

Dear Ones, in the Verses that follow Mystically we make the connection that we must not defile ourselves like the rest of the world. We are not like the rest of the world. We were designed to be different. We are designed to live Holy. Not only are we to guard all of the mitzvahs in the sense of carefully observing them, but we are to guard against any form of thought or instruction of eliminating them or superseding them! Observing the Commands are what makes us The People of Israel and what makes our land, Eretz Yisroel, the Holy Land!

Devarim 8.11

הִשָּׁמֶר לְךָ פֶּן־תִּשְׁכַּח אֶת־יְהֹוָה אֱלֹהֶיךָ לְבִלְתִּי **שְׁמֹר** מִצְוֹתָיו וּמִשְׁפָּטָיו וְחֻקֹּתָיו אֲשֶׁר אָנֹכִי מְצַוְּךָ הַיּוֹם:

Deuteronomy 8.11

You guard [The Commandments] in order not to forget everything from the Aleph to the Tav of The Lord your God. Do not [forget to] **keep** *His Commandments, and His Judgments, and His Statutes, which I Command you this day.*

Devarim 11.22

כִּי אִם־**שָׁמֹר** תִּשְׁמְרוּן אֶת־כָּל־הַמִּצְוָה הַזֹּאת אֲשֶׁר אָנֹכִי מְצַוֶּה אֶתְכֶם לַעֲשֹׂתָהּ לְאַהֲבָה אֶת־יְהֹוָה אֱלֹהֵיכֶם לָלֶכֶת בְּכָל־דְּרָכָיו וּלְדָבְקָה־בוֹ:

Deuteronomy 11.22

For if you shall diligently **keep** *everything*

from Aleph to Tav all these Commandments which I Command you, to do them, to love the Lord your God, to walk in all his ways, and to hold fast to him;

Training Children
Chapter 7

Parshat Kedoshim
Leviticus 19.1 - 20.27

Vayikra 19.3

אִישׁ אִמּוֹ וְאָבִיו תִּירָאוּ וְאֶת־שַׁבְּתֹתַי תִּשְׁמֹרוּ אֲנִי יְהוָה אֱלֹהֵיכֶם:

Leviticus 19.3
Man shall fear his Mother and his Father and everything from Aleph to Tav of keeping My Sabbaths; I am the Lord your God.

Why did our Creator place Sabbath alongside honoring one's Mother and Father? Are they connected? How are they connected? God Willing we are going to begin a gentle climb up to the answers over the entirety of this chapter.

Each of us are Children. This Chapter is about us. It is about our Parents who are children and their parents who are children and if we have children then our children who God Willing will have children. . In one way or another this is about everyone.

Our Creator allows many challenges. Sometimes the challenges seem insurmountable like climbing a great mountain, a 14,000 foot high mountain. Yet every mountain has a trail blazed to the top that can be conquered by steady, faithful diligence. In our Parshat this week we are considering the responsibility of honoring one's parents. Each of us has parents that we should honor. The Lord God places the Mitzvot / Observance of honoring parents as perhaps one of the most important Commandments written in Ha Torah. If an employer knew that the individual who they are considering for employment was disrespectful to her or his parents would that make a difference? SHOULD RESPECTING ONE'S PARENTS MAKE A DIFFERENCE TO AN EMPLOYER? If an institute were considering an application for a potential student should they be concerned if he or she was rude or impolite to his or her parents? SHOULD RESPECTING ONE'S

PARENTS MAKE A DIFFERENCE TO THE INSTITUTE OF HIGHER LEARNING? If a business owner were uncivil or insolent to the Mother or Father that labored to bring this child into the world and to provide for the child the best he or she could should this make a difference to his or her clients? SHOULD RESPECTING ONE'S PARENTS MAKE A DIFFERENCE TO CLIENTS OF THIS BUSINESS?

Let's consider these questions. Our country is governed by politicians who believe respect of parents is IMPORTANT! How do we know this? The news media zooms in on the lives of ones parents. The news media shows parents and family members sitting in the audience and on stage with their political daughter / son or relative. Why is it so important that the politician have the noticeable support of parents, spouse, family and relatives? This is supposed to send us a message of family unity and of parental approval of the child. Why do politicians speak of the labors of their fathers and mothers in their speeches? Well, if a politician cursed his or her parents or was rude or impolite to his or her parents how would this play out in the media? Politicians are fired by their supporters for marital infidelity all the time. So how well do you think political supporters would respond to parental abuse? Is it odd that so many Americans do not give high approval ratings to Congress or many political leaders? Many voters consider politicians to be liars... deceptive... dishonest... whether they are or not. Yet the men and women who run for office feel the need to show the world how much their parents support and believe in them. Are they trying to make a statement with us? Are they saying to the voters because my parents are in the audience and on the stage etc., you should trust me and you should vote for me because I am a good kid? I love and respect my parents. What is the message they are trying to convey?

If a man does not respect his mother will he respect his wife? If a woman does not respect her father will she respect her husband? If a man has issues with his parents will he have issues with his children? If a woman has issues with her parents will she have issues with her children?

CAN WE SEE HOW ALL OF THESE QUESTIONS RELATE?

If a man divorces his wife... if a woman divorces her husband... The children will be greatly impacted!! The husband / father will be impacted the wife / mother will be impacted each set of parents and relatives will be impacted.

EVERYTHING we have mentioned in this chapter thus far comes down to respect for parents.

All religions come together on this point. All beliefs teach RESPECT FOR PARENTS! This is a fundamental principle. Respect for parents is the foundation stone for every religion.

Having lived in the world before Torah Observance and then in the World after Torah Observance I saw the difference. I learned the difference. The difference is very great.

The Midrash shares a story of honoring ones parents. *R. Eliezer the Great was asked by his disciples: ' Can you give an example of [real] honoring of parents.' He replied: 'Go and see what Dama b. Nethina of Askelon did. His mother was mentally afflicted and she used to slap him in the presence of his colleagues, and all that he would say was, "Mother it is enough!"' Our Rabbis say: Once the Sages came to him to Askelon, where he lived, to buy from him a precious stone [to replace one] lost from the vestments of the [high] priest, and they fixed the price with him at a thousand golden pieces. He entered the house and found his father asleep with his leg stretched out on the chest wherein the stone was lying. He would not trouble him, and he came out empty-handed. As he did not produce the stone the Sages thought that he wanted a higher price, and they therefore raised their offer to ten thousand golden pieces. When his father awoke from his sleep Dama entered and brought out the stone. The Sages wished to give him ten thousand golden pieces, but he exclaimed: 'Heaven forfend! I will not make a profit out of honoring my parents; I will only take from you the first price, one thousand golden pieces, which I had fixed with you.' And what reward did the Holy One, blessed be He, give him? Our Rabbis report that in the very same year his cow gave birth to a red heifer which he sold for more than ten thousand golden pieces. From this we see how great the merit of honoring one's father and mother is.* Devarim Rabba 1.15

A man or woman that does not honor... esteem... hold in high regards his or her parents is an individual that is in serious trouble!!

Before we delve into the degree of trouble a child is in who does not respect both her or his mother and father we need to discuss the influence on a child from a divorced home. Sometimes a child is NOT at fault entirely. When the husband and wife divorce often children become victims of their parents and relatives revenge and rage. There is a story that is supposed to be humorous that helps to better explain this.

Two Jewish women were sitting next to each other under hair dryers at the hairdresser.

The first lady says, 'How's your family?'

The second lady responds, 'Just fine. It couldn't be better! She was so happy as she went on to share about her daughter. My daughter is married to the most wonderful man. She never has to cook, he always takes her out. She never has to clean, he got her a housekeeper. She never has to work, he's got such a good job. She never has to worry about the children, he got her a nanny. Life couldn't be any better for her.'

The second lady ask the first lady, 'So how about you? How is your son these days?'

The first lady says, 'Awful. It couldn't be worse... My son is married to such a witch of a woman. She makes him take her out to dinner every night. She never sets a foot in their new kitchen. She made Sam get her a housekeeper, God Forbid that she should vacuum a carpet or clean one of their five bathrooms. He has to work so long and hard. Why? Because that little princess will not get a job. With all her bridge parties she never takes the time to care for their children. She demanded that my son hire a butler and a nanny. They live in the servants quarters at the back of the house. Life is horrible for him. Life could not be any worse for my son...'

Then they got from underneath their hair dryers and realized that...

Even though this couple was married and living together we see the same story as told from two completely different positions. The stories are so different it is difficult to believe they were speaking of the same two people. Divorce can be somewhat like this. Rebbetzin Revi shares the story of when she went to spend a few weeks with her Father and Step Mother. Her Mother acted let's say unfriendly towards her for several weeks before and after the visit. This was unfortunate. Yet children from divorced parents experience much worse than this. Children of difficult divorces are placed in situations where they frequently must choose sides. Often friends and relatives line up on one side or the other. They pressure the children! They teach the children to disrespect either their Mother or father. Sometimes friends and relatives just look the other way instead of encouraging the children to do Biblically what is right. **This is WRONG!! This is a violation of the basic principle in every religion of honoring ones parents!!** Any mother or father, grand parent, relative or friend who encourages a child to do anything less than honor their mother and father is in deep trouble with The Creator. I understand that there are places in life's road where parents maybe unfit due to drugs, alcohol abuse mental illness yet this is NOT an opening for disrespecting ones Mother or Father. Often parents are of different religious belief's. My first wife professes Christianity. I profess Judaism. Neither of our sons are Jewish because their mother is not Jewish. I am not sure what my sons believe even though we have discussed this subject. They are adults who choose to live in isolation to their father. Dear Readers, there is a place and a time when the influence of mother or father, friends or relatives can no longer be an excuse for not communicating with one's Mother or Father. There is a line that can be crossed by children after they become adults. Adult children who choose not to honor their Mother or Father in such circumstances may be held accountable by The Lord God for their disrespectful actions. It is not my place to Judge. Judgment belongs to The Lord God!

We have just discussed a few of the many possibilities that may result from children from divorced parents.

It is understandable why a Mother or Father would be concerned with allowing children under 18 to be close to a parent that used drugs, alcohol or who was mental ill. Yet there comes a time when the child is responsible for their actions. I encourage children and parents who are struggling with these types of issues to contact me. I am not a psychologist or a family counselor. I am a concerned parent who can empathize with you.

Most religions teach their followers to marry within their religion. This is understandable. It is also understandable that divorced parents may pressure children to believe as they do. Children may desire to believe differently. It is understandable for one parent to be very concerned about allowing their children to have close contact with a Mother or Father of a different belief. Yet, teaching or encouraging children any form of disrespect to their Mother or

Father is WRONG by the beliefs and standards of most religions. Young children maybe prohibited from close contact with a parent under such circumstances yet this should not result in any form of disrespect to either of their parents. **Encouraging any form of disrespect to parents is a SIN that both the parent and child will suffer from. Anyone that encourages children to disrespect their parents will held accountable by The Lord God in the Day of Judgment for such actions!**

Before my Father died there were several periods of time when it was necessary to pull the plug on our communication. My Father may he rest in peace, was a devout Pentecostal Christian and retired Pastor. My Father did a great deal of good in this world yet he also did some things that were toxic. He would send Christian Messianic missionaries by our home to try and convert us to Christianity. This is what Christians do. Often the conversations between Daddy and me would lead to a strong condemnation of me and my wife for not believing in Jesus etc. We would be reminded that we were going to burn in hell for eternity etc. as only my Father could do. Recently one of my Brothers who is a Pentecostal Christian Pastor said to me three times in our phone conversation that Jesus Christ was his lord and savior. I knew what his beliefs were. This is not the first time he has shared them with me. Was it necessary for him to repeat Jesus Christ was his lord and savior three times? No! But, he did it any way. This resulted in me challenging his doctrines and eventually a disconnect etc. I wish my behavior during this conversation was calmer. There is no excuse for me raising my voice even though I have been challenged many times by relatives about my faith.

Dear Reader, I understand what Christians believe. I graduated from Christian Bible School and Seminary. Yet, my brother felt this need to whack me. This is what Christians do! My youngest brother is a Pentecostal Christian Pastor. He told me I am a reprobate and that I was going to burn in hell if I did not believe in Jesus.

I have asked sincere questions, hard questions for Christians to answer about what the Bible Teaches to my Father when he was a live and to both of my brothers. To this date they have not answered my questions. They cannot read Hebrew. They do not know anything about the 613 Commands of Ha Torah. HERE is the key - They have limited interest in the TRUTH. Their interest lies in what they believe. They are afraid to be challenged. I understand why they are fearful. I have some very challenging questions that they cannot answer. I have asked these questions many times to many Christians and am still waiting for an answer for over 20 years... My Father said that I was too educated. He would say things like, look at all these Christian scholars, are you telling me they are wrong? I stopped communicating with my Father because he was toxic. This means he was degrading, insulting and speaking with him unhealthy. My brothers have stopped communicating with me. Nether has given me the courtesy of saying why. When my Father would phone we would talk. As soon as the communication headed in the direction of being degrading, insulting or his condemnations I would say Daddy we need to change the subject. If we do not change the subject I am going to have to conclude this conversation. Daddy I don't want to hang up on you but...

Dear Reader, it is not alright for a parent to be abusive with their child. A parent should not be physically abusive or verbally abusive. My Father was both physically abusive and verbally abusive when I was growing up even though he did not normally use vulgar language. Unfortunately I followed in his foot steps. As a Father I was physically abusive and verbally abusive to my oldest son. I was verbally abusive to both sons. I get it! I understand why they want nothing to do with me. However after returning to Judaism I have begun a slow dedicated reversal from past mistakes and improper actions. It won't help my wrongful actions but it may be helpful to others who are walking that awful path. I wrote a book in 2013 entitled *Eve of Creation RESTORED*. This is a really good book about how to heal relationships. I am not an expert. I have many failings but through all my failings I have learned and improved. In the Forward on the book my wife Revi does not paint me as a perfect husband. I am a man who is driving in reverse of former poor choices. I have a long ways to back up. My hope is in being able to help anyone who is following the destructive path I followed.

I have reached out to my sons. The ball is in their court. My sons know what I believe. It is not necessary for me to communicate what I believe to them. If they choose to have a relationship with their dad down the road that would be fine. If they choose not to have that relationship I understand but I don't think our loving Creator will accept their excuses. Why? Our Creator Forgives us of our every sin when we acknowledge our sin, when we make a plan to reverse our poor actions and when we follow that plan and if we are willing to pay for damages we caused. These are the standards The Lord God holds all of us to. The Lord God is very forgiving and we must also learn to be forgiving.

I would like to say a word to any Christians who reads this book. I have met many very fine

Christian folk. They truly believe in and practice God's Love. They turn the other cheek. They help the poor. They walk the extra mile. They have said more to me through their actions of kindness than all the preachers shouting from their stages... I know what they believe. They know what I believe. We have not shouted at each other or shared in any remarks of condemnation. It is possible for people of very different beliefs to work together on many common goals to make a big difference in our world.

While writing this book we learned that my dearest wife Revi had cancer. Revi and I contacted relatives including my two brothers. To the best of our knowledge everyone in our families that we contacted responded with love and kindness and words of encouragement except for my brothers... Now one would think that there would be Christian love and understanding... Perhaps actions like these are the reasons religions fought crusades and may again...

Yet I have light neither of them posses. I must be

tolerant and understanding and compassionate. For some of us this is not our finest quality. Yet we have to bury all these hurt feeling and let them go just as if nothing had happened. We have to be ready to reach out in a minute in love when the opportunity arises. Why? Jews are the Light of the world. We are the chosen people. Our land is the Holy land. We are the ones who are suppose to make a difference.

This brings us to another important point in Honoring one's Mother and Father. It's being consistent. Our children pick up our lack of good judgment, our exceptions, our reasons why we do not follow what the Bible Teaches... Then later down the road we wonder just where did they get this lack of respect from...

I would like to say a word to former Christians who feel duped by Christianity... Pastors... Teachers etc. Please stop using xtian when you write. it is insulting. It is not following the standard of Love our Creator expects from us no matter how unhappy... bitter... and angry we may be. I struggled with these same issues. Then one day a friend wrote to me. He made a few points about how I need to change my attitude. This was wise counsel. Remember Christians do what Christians do. Who can we get angry with them for the same things that we used to do? We really need a lot of patience, compassion, understanding, kindness and love in our dealings with them.

We have spent a number of pages discussing issues regarding honoring ones Mother and Father. There is an important connection to honoring ones parents that is connected to Sabbath.

Vayikra 19.3

אִישׁ אִמּוֹ וְאָבִיו תִּירָאוּ וְאֶת־שַׁבְּתֹתַי תִּשְׁמֹרוּ אֲנִי יְהוָה אֱלֹהֵיכֶם:

Leviticus 19.3

Man shall fear his Mother and his Father and everything from Aleph to Tav of keeping My Sabbaths; I am the Lord your God.

Why did our Creator place Sabbath alongside honoring one's Mother and Father? Are they connected? How are they connected? There are many connections. The first and most important is We know God through honoring our parents. Mystically we know that Aleph equals 1,000. The Gematria of אִישׁ אִמּוֹ וְאָבִיו תִּירָאוּ / Eesh Eemoh Vih Aw Vee Tee Raw Voo meaning Man shall fear his Mother and his Father is the Gematria of 1,000.

אִישׁ אִמּוֹ וְאָבִיו תִּירָאוּ
Eesh Eemoh Vih Aw Vee Tee Raw Voo
Man shall fear his Mother and his Father
383 = 6ו 10י 2ב 1א 6ו 6ו 40מ 1א 300ש 10י 1א
617 = 6ו 1א 200ר 10י 400ת
1000 = 383 + 617

1 = א
Aleph = 1000

When on honers ones parents like Dama b. Nethina of Askelon it pays great dividends. We see these dividends in the Letter Aleph which is One but means one thousand.

Shemot 20.8

זָכוֹר אֶת־יוֹם הַשַׁבָּת לְקַדְּשׁוֹ:

Exodus 20.8
Remember everything from Aleph to Tav of the Sabbath Day to keep it Holy.

יוֹם הַשַׁבָּת
Yom Ha Shah bawth / The Day Sabbath
י 10 ו 6 מ 40   ה 5 ש 300 ב 2 ת 400 = 763

וַהֲשֵׁיבֹתָם
Vah Hah Shay Yov Tehm
And Return them
ו 6 ה 5 ש 300 י 10 ב 2 ת 400 מ 40 = 763

Honoring ones parents and Sabbath are connected. We refer to Sabbath as The Sabbath Day. We do not say the Sabbath days. Sabbath is one day from a week of seven Days. We begin with the first day, then the second day, then the third day, then the fourth day, then the fifth day, then the sixth day to arrive at the Seventh day. Once one Observes a single solitary Sabbath each Sabbath after the first is a return to the

Sabbath Day this began. Mystically when we combine the Gematria of 1000 with our Gematria of 763 we observe that there are great rewards for the one who returns to Observe the Sabbath Day. The same great rewards apply to the one who respects their Mother and their Father. We arrive at the Gematria of 1000 by having a great respect for our Mother and Father. The point is that there is power in observing just one Sabbath. When one Observes one Sabbath they are challenged to return to a second Sabbath and a third. Therefore one is returning to them. In the same way as one returns to Sabbath again and again one must return to Her / His parents time and again. Remembering the Sabbath and honoring ones parents both bring rewards. Also just as one is to remember the Sabbath Day one is to remember one's Parents. We are required to honor parents and we are required to honor The Sabbath Day to keep it Holy to keep it separated. Just as we begin ascending the seven stairs, i.e. each day of the week to ascend to The Sabbath Day, i.e. the Pinnacle of the week one parents are to be elevated. Just as one is to hold The Sabbath Day in High esteem one is to hold their parents in High Esteem.

We could just as easily say Honor the Sabbath Day to Keep it Holy... Children observe the manner in which a parent observes Sabbath.

If a parent downplays the separation of Sabbath from the other six days of the week, in actuality the parent is teaching the children that complete honor of Sabbaths as taught in Ha Torah is not required. As a result, the children learn the definition of honor from their parent's example. In return, unfortunately, the children will honor their parents in the same fashion the parents honor Sabbath. Improper observance of Sabbath makes a strong impression upon our children just as diligent, careful observance of Sabbath does.

Parents we can introduce life and happiness into children's lives. We can teach them how to honor us by our example of our honoring of the Sabbath or we can scatter stumbling blocks throughout their lives that makes honoring Sabbath and honoring parents difficult. We can plant and cultivate controversy in our children's lives, by our lack of Sabbath Observance or our improper Observances, God forbid! Our children will be held to account for their own actions regardless of the conflicts imposed upon them from their families.

Our children are not released from Torah Observance, from honoring Sabbath or from honoring parents just because we as parents blew it. So we must be very careful.

Rashi says, that Keeping the Sabbath is placed adjacent to the fear of your father and mother in order to Teach us: even though I warned you regarding the fear of one's Father and one's Mother, if he / she should say to you: 'Violate the Sabbath,' you must not listen to her / him - and also in regard to all the other *mitzvot* of Ha Torah.

The first step is to restore true Sabbath observance is to make an attempt! Restore the Sabbath Observance robbed from you by former generations! Restore the Sabbath experience in its fullness. Return to higher ground! Restore the Holy Honor of Sabbath in your life. Make an effort to Restore Sabbath.

When I rediscovered Sabbath the storms surrounding my life did not immediately clear up. In fact the storms became much greater. Yet within these mighty storms was a day of tranquility, a day of rest, a day set aside from all the other days each week.

Years of non Jewish learning muddies the waters. Much sorting out has to be done. It takes weeks, months, years and possibly a lifetime to work through all the conflicts! Yet for the Jew who reestablishes Sabbath Observance there is a break in the conflict! There is a path to follow!

Now I look back with understanding and with more clarity. I clung to the only path that was revealed to me. I clung to Sabbath. The revelation of Sabbath eventually led me out of mighty storms to more and greater Torah Observances. It is my prayer that Sabbath Observance will do the same for those who are struggling with family issues. May our Creator Bless you with greater Sabbath Observances. There is never an end to the greatness of Sabbath!

Defining Holiness
Chapter 8

Parshat Emor
Leviticus 21.1 - 24.23

Vayikra 22.32

וְלֹא תְחַלְלוּ אֶת־שֵׁם קָדְשִׁי וְנִקְדַּשְׁתִּי בְּתוֹךְ בְּנֵי יִשְׂרָאֵל אֲנִי יְהֹוָה מְקַדִּשְׁכֶם:

Leviticus 22.32
You shall not profane My Holy Name but I will be sanctified among, The People of Israel. I am The Lord Who makes you Holy.

Within our universe there seems to be a misconception of what it means to be Holy. We must consider the questions: What is Holy? What is Holiness? Who defines what Holy means? Does it matter who defines the meaning of Holiness?

So often we look so holy with our long black coats, our black hats, our black kippot, our short hair, our payot, our long dresses, our sheitels, our outward actions, our Sabbath attendance, our davening and many other outward appearances. The problem with outward appearances is that too often they are sadly founded on showtime pretenses. They are not real. Good habits are important. And they are healthy. Yet, to suggest that smoking and drinking among other habits are the soil for sinners is wrong. In fact, Rabbi Shlomo Carlebach, may he rest in peace, related the story of the Shwartzah Wolf as told to the Belzer Rebbe by the great grandson. He related the story.

There was a man who for many years had no children. And the gates of heaven were closed to him and his wife. This man was instructed to get a Bracha from the Shwartzah Wolf. Why? The Shwartzah Wolf was the head of the thirty-six Tzaddikim, the Shwartzah Wolf was the only one who could open the gates of Heaven. [We teach that our world exists because of the pure and righteous acts of thirty-six righteous people in every generation.]

The Shwartzah Wolf, a woodcutter living in the forest. He isolated himself. He was a very unpopular Jew in the community. He was described as being obnoxious. And his wife's words and his children's actions could not be repeated. This is a man who was not given an Aliyah at the community shul and for whose funeral the men of the shul did not want to make a minyan. Yet he was the head of the thirty-six Tzaddikim, the only one who could open the gates of Heaven. How could this be?

This desperate individual devised a plan to obtain the blessing from the Shwartzah Wolf. He would appear at the Shwartzah Wolf's home as a Jew acting lost in the forest shortly before Sabbath. His thinking was, 'They will be forced to offer me accommodations.' He knocked on the door. The wife of the Shwartzah Wolf appeared at the door, so ugly, so vial, so intimidating. The children behind her appeared mean like little devils. The house was in disarray, unkept and untidy. The home of the tzaddik felt like a scary place.

The Yid said, 'I'm lost in the forest, Sabbath is about to begin, may I please stay at your house?'

She cursed at him and directed him to the barn where he could sleep on the hay. She warned him that if he came near the house during Sabbath her husband would kill him.

Late that evening, the Shwartzah Wolf appeared before him in the barn and warned him, 'I expect you to be gone two minutes after Sabbath is over. Don't open the door to my house or I'll kill you with my bare hands.

The Yid was terrified. This is not quite what he envisioned. He was a dead man. His wife would be childless. The Shwartzah Wolf would not give him the Bracha. The gates of Heaven would remain closed. Then late on Sabbath afternoon he began to cry Tears rolled down his cheeks as he sat in the barn among the cows of the Shwartzah Wolf. He fell to his knees there in the barn, openly sobbing out of control as he remembered his tears could open the gates of Heaven. It was at that time that the barn door flew open and there stood the Shwartzah Wolf, brightly shining as if he were the High Priest. He invited him to the third meal of Sabbath, Shalosh Seudot.

They entered the home together. The wife of the Shwartzah Wolf was exquisitely beautiful, the children were well behaved and adorable, shining bright like little priests. The house was immaculate and tidy like the Bet HaMikdash.

The Shwartzah Wolf said, 'I know why you have come, and the gates of Heaven are open to you.. I grant you your request. I bless you with a son. I have only one request, that you name him after me.'

The Yid trembled with excitement as he traveled home to share the good news with his wife...The next morning while in shul he learned that the Shwartzah Wolf had died, may he rest in peace.

Reb Shlomo goes on to explain that a Tzaddik like The Shwartzah Wolf is a mirror that reflects our own neshama. So if we use inappropriate language or if our behavior is obnoxious then the Tzaddik only mirrors what we truly are. The Tzaddik does NOT mirror what we appear to be or what others think we are. On the other hand, if we are Holy, the Tzaddik mirrors that Holiness.

So the point is real Holiness may NOT be based on the conformity of how one dresses or if one lives in a community or one's education or one's position in the community. The Tzaddik could be the woodcutter in the wilderness who cannot bear community incongruity. It gives us something to think about...

A staff member at JewishPath.org was sharing notes from a class that he attended. The class leader was discussing a Jew's responsibility to live by Ha Torah's Definition of what it means to be Jewish. This discussion was in an Orthodox shul to Orthodox Jews. The class leader stated that Jews who dress "LIKE" frum Jews need to live within Ha Torah's Definition / expectation of frumkeit!

In the same way, the world needs to understand what Holiness is and who defines what Holiness is. Holiness is not up for personal interpretation. Holiness was predefined before the Creation of man or religion. Holiness was defined by The Lord God!

1 Samuel 2.2
There is none Holy as The Lord for there is none besides You neither is there any Rock like our God.

The Torah clearly States that The Lord Expects The People of Yisroel, / Kal Yisroel / all of Yisroel to be Holy! Why?

Leviticus 19.2
Speak to all the congregation of the people of Israel, and say to them, You shall be Holy; for I the Lord your God Am Holy.

Leviticus 20.26
And you shall be Holy to me; for I the Lord

am Holy, and have separated you from other people, that you should be mine.

Leviticus 21.8
You shall make him {the Kohen} Holy {even against his will, Rashi} {WHY?} for he offers the bread of your God; **He shall be Holy unto you** *{WHY?} for* **I, The Lord, am Holy, Who Makes you Holy.**

Again, the point is The Lord Expects Kal Yisroel to be Holy! Why? The People of Israel are called by His Name...

2 Chronicles 7.14
If My people, who are called by My Name, shall humble themselves, and pray, and seek My face, and turn from their wicked ways; then will I hear from heaven, and will forgive their sin, and will heal their land.

Leviticus 22.2
Speak to Aharon and to his sons and let them keep away from the Holy Offerings of The People of Israel {on the days of their

impurities, Rashi} *and they shall not profane My Holy Name which they sanctify for Me, I am The Lord.*

Leviticus 22.32
You shall not profane My Holy Name but I will be sanctified among, The People of Israel. I am The Lord Who makes you Holy.

This tells us something about a Jew's responsibility. **We are NOT TO PROFANE The Lord's Holy Name! Instead we are to SANCTIFY The Lord'S HOLY NAME! No other people or religion are given this great and Holy responsibility! Only The People of Yisroel are held responsible to SANCTIFY The Lord's HOLY NAME!** So how do we fulfill our important responsibility? What is our guideline? The Torah of The Lord is our guide.

Dear Reader, ONLY THE TORAH DEFINES what the Jew's responsibility of Holiness is. Holy reader, ONLY THE TORAH DEFINES what The Lord Deems as Holy.

Exodus 19.6
And you shall be to me a kingdom of priests, and a holy nation. These are the words which you shall speak to the people of Israel.

Exodus 20.8
Remember the Sabbath day, to keep it holy.

Exodus 26.34
And you shall put the covering upon the Ark of the Testimony in the most Holy Place.

Holy Garments Ex. 28.2, the Holy Offering, the Holy Gifts Ex. 28.38, the Holy Crown, Ex. 29.6, the Holy Altar Ex. 29.37, the Holy Ointment, the Holy Anointing oil Ex. 30.25, the Holy Rim Ex. 39.30, the Holy Mishkon, the Holy Utensils Ex. 40.9, the Holy Offerings Lev. 2.3, the Holy Crown Lev. 8.9, the Holy Linen Coat Lev. 16.3, the Holy Sanctuary Lev. 16.33, the Holy Fruit Lev. 19.24, the Holy Things Lev. 22.2, the Holy Name Lev. 22.32, the Holy Gathering Lev. 23.2 and many, many, more items and degrees of Holiness.

Now, holy reader, please realize that for these reasons and many others Ha Torah is very well and very, very alive, THANK God! Also please realize that while other people and other religions may sanctify The Lord's Holy Name at their choice, ONLY KAL YISROEL ARE COMMANDED AND REQUIRED BY The Lord TO DO SO! It is a very, very serious responsibility to be chosen for such an important task! Not only is the responsibility very important but the Book, the Torah, which instructs us in fulfilling these responsibilities is also extremely IMPORTANT! The Torah is our guide! No other book has replaced our Torah!!

Our Sages Teach that every Jew is Holy. Our Holiness is Echad / One! We we are not one individual but we are one. Kal Yisroel / All Yisroel are Echad as one. We are a kingdom of priests. We Kal Yisroel as Echad are a Holy Nation. The Gematria for 'Kal Yisroel' is 591. The Gematria for Ah Nee The Lord Mi Kah Deesh Chem {meaning 'I am The Lord Who makes you [Kal Yisroel] Holy.' is also 591. So from this we Mystically learn that it is The Lord that chooses, requires and makes Kal Yisroel Holy, and it is Ha Torah that Teaches Kal Yisroel to differentiate between Holy and unholy, and between clean and unclean.

Vayikra 31.13

וְאַתָּה דַּבֵּר אֶל־בְּנֵי יִשְׂרָאֵל לֵאמֹר אַךְ אֶת־שַׁבְּתֹתַי תִּשְׁמֹרוּ כִּי אוֹת הִוא בֵּינִי וּבֵינֵיכֶם לְדֹרֹתֵיכֶם לָדַעַת כִּי אֲנִי יְהוָֹה מְקַדִּשְׁכֶם :

Shemot 31.13
Speak you also to the people of Israel, saying, Truly My Sabbaths you shall keep; for it is a sign between me and you throughout your generations; that you may know that I am the Lord that does sanctify you.

כָּל־יִשְׂרָאֵל
Kal Yisroel / All of Israel
כ 20 ל 30   י 10 ש 300 ר 200 א 1 ל 30 = 591

אֲנִי יְהוָה מְקַדִּשְׁכֶם
Ah Nee   The Lord   Mi Kah Deesh Chem
I am The Lord which Makes You Holy
87 = 5ה 6ו 5ה 10י   10י 50נ 1א
504 = 40ם 20כ 300ש 4ד 100ק 40מ
591 = 87 + 504

Gematria Tefillin 570
Chapter 9

Parshat Behar
Leviticus 25.1 - 26.2

Vayikra 25.10

וְקִדַּשְׁתֶּם אֵת שְׁנַת הַחֲמִשִּׁים שָׁנָה וּקְרָאתֶם דְּרוֹר בָּאָרֶץ לְכָל־יֹשְׁבֶיהָ **יוֹבֵל הִוא תִּהְיֶה לָכֶם** וְשַׁבְתֶּם אִישׁ אֶל־אֲחֻזָּתוֹ וְאִישׁ אֶל־מִשְׁפַּחְתּוֹ תָּשֻׁבוּ׃

Leviticus 25.10

And you shall hallow the fiftieth year, and proclaim liberty throughout all the land to all the inhabitants of it; **it shall be a Jubilee to you;** *and you shall return every man to his possession, and you shall return every man to his family.*

In our discussion we are going to try and work out way up to the Year of Jubilee.

The Gematria of 570 is among one of my favorites. From early in the days when I returned to Yiddishkeit I have deeply cherished its special message.

In the Shema we {the Jewish men from thirteen years and up} are Commanded by God in Ha Torah, 'Place these words of Mine upon your heart and upon your soul; bind them for a sign upon your arm and let them be Tefillin between your eyes...'

Devarim 11.13 - 21

וְהָיָה אִם־שָׁמֹעַ תִּשְׁמְעוּ אֶל־מִצְוֹתַי אֲשֶׁר אָנֹכִי מְצַוֶּה אֶתְכֶם הַיּוֹם לְאַהֲבָה אֶת־יְהוָֹה אֱלֹהֵיכֶם וּלְעָבְדוֹ בְּכָל־לְבַבְכֶם וּבְכָל־נַפְשְׁכֶם: וְנָתַתִּי מְטַר־אַרְצְכֶם בְּעִתּוֹ יוֹרֶה וּמַלְקוֹשׁ וְאָסַפְתָּ דְגָנֶךָ וְתִירֹשְׁךָ וְיִצְהָרֶךָ: וְנָתַתִּי עֵשֶׂב בְּשָׂדְךָ לִבְהֶמְתֶּךָ וְאָכַלְתָּ וְשָׂבָעְתָּ: הִשָּׁמְרוּ לָכֶם פֶּן־יִפְתֶּה לְבַבְכֶם וְסַרְתֶּם וַעֲבַדְתֶּם אֱלֹהִים אֲחֵרִים וְהִשְׁתַּחֲוִיתֶם לָהֶם: וְחָרָה אַף־יְהוָֹה בָּכֶם וְעָצַר אֶת־הַשָּׁמַיִם וְלֹא־יִהְיֶה מָטָר וְהָאֲדָמָה לֹא תִתֵּן אֶת־יְבוּלָהּ וַאֲבַדְתֶּם מְהֵרָה מֵעַל הָאָרֶץ הַטֹּבָה אֲשֶׁר יְהוָֹה נֹתֵן לָכֶם: וְשַׂמְתֶּם אֶת־דְּבָרַי אֵלֶּה עַל־לְבַבְכֶם וְעַל־נַפְשְׁכֶם וּקְשַׁרְתֶּם אֹתָם לְאוֹת עַל־יֶדְכֶם וְהָיוּ לְטוֹטָפֹת בֵּין עֵינֵיכֶם: וְלִמַּדְתֶּם אֹתָם אֶת־בְּנֵיכֶם לְדַבֵּר בָּם בְּשִׁבְתְּךָ בְּבֵיתֶךָ וּבְלֶכְתְּךָ בַדֶּרֶךְ

וּבְשָׁכְבְּךָ וּבְקוּמֶךָ: וּכְתַבְתָּם עַל־מְזוּזוֹת בֵּיתֶךָ וּבִשְׁעָרֶיךָ:
לְמַעַן יִרְבּוּ יְמֵיכֶם וִימֵי בְנֵיכֶם עַל הָאֲדָמָה אֲשֶׁר נִשְׁבַּע
יְהֹוָה לַאֲבֹתֵיכֶם לָתֵת לָהֶם כִּימֵי הַשָּׁמַיִם עַל־הָאָרֶץ:

Deuteronomy 11.13 - 21

And it shall come to pass, if you shall give heed diligently to my Commandments which I command you this day, to love the Lord your God, and to serve him with all your heart and with all your soul. That I will give you the rain of your land in its due season, the first rain and the latter rain, that you may gather in your grain, and your wine, and your oil. And I will send grass in your fields for your cattle, that you may eat and be full. Take heed to yourselves, that your heart be not deceived, and you turn aside, and serve other gods, and worship them; And then the Lord's anger be kindled against you, and he closed the skies, that there should be no rain, and that the land yield not her fruit; and lest you perish quickly from off the good land which the Lord gives you. Therefore shall you lay up these my words in your heart and in your soul, and **bind them for a sign upon your hand, that they may be as frontlets between your eyes.** *And you shall teach them to your children, speaking of them when you sit in your house, and when you walk by the way, when you lie down, and when you rise up. And you shall write them upon the door posts of your house, and upon your gates; That your days may be multiplied, and the days of your children, in the land which the Lord swore to your fathers to give them, as the days of heaven upon the earth.*

In our daily prayer Siddurs Artscroll translates the word לְטוֹטָפֹת Lih Toh Taw Poht meaning frontlets as תְּפִלִּין **Tefillin.** Rabbi Menachem Davis, Editor, The Shottenstein Edition Siddur for Weekdays, (Brooklyn, NY: Mesorah Publications, Ltd., First Edition, 2002), p 134 **The Gematria of** לְטוֹטָפֹת **is 534.**

Each morning at the time of prayer, Shacharit, we don our Tefillin with special blessings. It is a routine, a good routine. It is a habit, a good habit. But wearing Tefillin is more than that. I don't suppose that those who wear Tefillin have ever felt the HEAVY WEIGHT of the obligation of fulfilling the mitzvah. Wearing Tefillin is a sign. It is a sign of the generations passed from Father to son to grandson. It is a sign of responsibility! It is a sign of maturity. It is a sign of one's Jewishness. It is also a sign of Gematria.

The Gematria of Tefillin is 570.

תְּפִלִּין
Tefillin
570 = 50נ 10י 30ל 80פ 400ת

One should note that any challenge to not wear their Tefillin comes from Yetzer Raw, meaning evil inclination. I do not designate or preface evil inclination with the letter ה 'Hey' meaning 'the', as some do, because using the letter in front of Yetzer Raw designates the word with a definite article. Having the Yetzer Raw / Evil inclination is difficult enough. Why would any of us want to lay the royal carpet in front of the Yetzer Raw. Why classify the evil inclination with a definite article? My Rabbi argues with my 'grammar' here. With due respect of this objection, there are many variations in Hebrew Letters and Words and I think this should be one of them. Why should the word Yetzer Raw receive the same honor given to other names and titles? Why should my personal tester - my יצר רע Yetzer Raw / Evil inclination receive the Letter Hey if front of it? I argue, It should NOT! The Gematria for Yetzer Raw is 570.

יצר רע
Yetzer Raw / Evil inclination
570 = 70ע 200ר   200ר 90צ 10י

In the Midrash evil inclination is written often as / יצר רע **Yetzer Raw.** We should also note that the God given responsibility of Yetzer Raw is to test us. Our father Avraham Aveinu was tested Yeh Sehr meaning "Ten" {times} He passed each test, thank God! The Gematria for ten is 570.

עֶשֶׂר
Eh Sehr
570 = 200ר 300שׂ 70ע

Unfortunately there are times in life where we are forced to face an evil man, an evil person. To say they are unpleasant to deal with does not come close to the level of frustration they attempt to invoke. That individual is NOT Yetzer Raw. That person is Raw Shaw, meaning evil / wicked. There is a difference between the two. One is a tester sent to test and strengthen us, the other is a destroyer sent to ruin us, God Forbid! We deal with both in the same manner. We don our royal crown. We don our Tefillin. Our Tefillin is the sign that we are obedient to our King, The Lord, and His Commands and His Torah. We wrap our weaker hand and arm with Tefillin as a form of "SPIRITUAL ARMOR" and by fulfilling the Commandment of Tefillin we defeat Yetzer Raw and Raw Shaw, thank God. The Gematria for Raw Shaw is 570.

רָשָׁע
Raw Shaw
570 = 70ע 300שׁ 200ר

Vayikra 25.10

וְקִדַּשְׁתֶּם אֵת שְׁנַת הַחֲמִשִּׁים שָׁנָה וּקְרָאתֶם דְּרוֹר בָּאָרֶץ

לְכָל־יֹשְׁבֶיהָ יוֹבֵל הִוא תִּהְיֶה לָכֶם וְשַׁבְתֶּם אִישׁ אֶל־אֲחֻזָּתוֹ וְאִישׁ אֶל־מִשְׁפַּחְתּוֹ תָּשֻׁבוּ:

Leviticus 25.10

And you shall hallow the fiftieth year, and proclaim liberty throughout all the land to all the inhabitants of it; it shall be a jubilee to you; and you shall return every man to his possession, and you shall return every man to his family.

יוֹבֵל הִוא תִּהְיֶה לָכֶם
Law Chem Yoh Vayl Hee Tee Hih Yeh
It shall be for you a Jubilee
60 = א1 ו6 ה5   ל30 ב2 ו6 י10
510 = ם40 כ20 ל30   ה5 י10 ה5 ת400
570 = 60 + 510

Now there is much, much more to the Gematria 570 including but not limited to Yoh Vahl Hee Tee Yeh Law Chem, meaning *'It shall be for you a Jubilee.'* Leviticus 25.10. In other words, wearing Tefillin is an expression of freedom. Wearing Tefillin expresses honor to the halachas of Shemittat Karka'ot (the Sabbatical year as regards agricultural work in Eretz Yisroel). Observing the mitzvah of putting the Tefillin on, which is like the accumulation of seven Sabbatical years {7 x 7 = 49} in that it is approaching the fiftieth year, the year of Jubilee, just as wearing Tefillin is a spiritual act whereby one elevates towards the fiftieth level. Wearing Tefillin is an expression of our superiority over Yetzer Raw and Raw Shaw.

There are many other expressions that reinforce the powerful sign of donning Tefillin and reciting the Shema and Shemoneh Esrei. This is a very deep subject!

Rev Shlomo Carlebach related the following story at the Lubavitcher Rebbe's funeral. He said that *there was no distance between the Rebbe and every other Jew in the world. He said when one would come before the Rebbe that the Rebbe knows you. He knows you in this life or in a previous life.* Rebbe Shlomo said that while doing a concert in Israel a non religious Yid came up to him. They talked. He was becoming reform. Shlomo asked him a question. *What turned you on?*

He said, *I got divorced. My children don't talk to me. I feel very lonely. I have children. Then one morning there's a bang on his door. He opens the door and two Yidden with beards are standing outside.*

They said to him, *We are coming to you in the name of the Lubavitcher Rebbe. He wants you to put on the Tefilin.*

The man says, *What? The Lubavitcher Rebbe wants me to put on Tefilin. He thinks, Hummmm... There is a Yid in the world that cares so much for me that he wants me to put on Tefillin.* Dear Reader the Lubavitcher Rebbe knew the power of wearing Tefillin.

Yid I would really appreciate it if you would join with me by sharing in the mitzvah of putting on Tefilin...

Remember My Holy Land!
Chapter 10

Parshat Bechukosai
Leviticus 26.3 - 27.34

Vayikra 26.43
וְהָאָרֶץ תֵּעָזֵב מֵהֶם וְתִרֶץ אֶת־שַׁבְּתֹתֶיהָ בָּהְשַׁמָּה מֵהֶם וְהֵם יִרְצוּ אֶת־עֲוֺנָם יַעַן וּבְיַעַן בְּמִשְׁפָּטַי מָאָסוּ וְאֶת־חֻקֹּתַי גָּעֲלָה נַפְשָׁם׃

Leviticus 26.43
The land, being bereft of them, will be appeased for its Sabbaths, during the time of its desolation from them and their iniquities will then be appeased {forgiven} since what certainly caused {this} is that they despised My laws and their soul loathed {rejected} My statutes.

The Lord made these Comments in reference to His faithfulness to His Covenant with The People of Israel. We failed to keep the Sabbatical year and Sabbaths because we despised His Laws.

In this week's Parshat we read The Lord's Words, 'I Will Remember.' We also read, 'and I Will Remember the land.' Leviticus 26.42

Years ago I was approached by a man while I was waiting in a shopping store checkout line. He was not Messianic even though he carried Messianic literature. He was not mean. He was friendly! He was attempting to make conversation with me about the Bible. He was observant to his Christian doctrine as expressed in Mark 16:15.16,

Mark writes that Christians are to '...*Go into all the world, and preach the gospel to every creature. And he that believes and is baptized shall be saved; but he that does believe shall be damned.* {also Matthew 28:19,20 and Acts 1:18 plus...}

Ha Torah does NOT Teach this!!

I was in a hurry! My time was very tight. That is often the situation when I'm out and about. Yet The Lord allowed the man to approach me. I felt like looking up and shouting, 'Why now? I'm very busy! This man is not Jewish. He is not a Messianic. I have no responsibility to speak with him.' Or... do I? Evidently I did.

As we stood in line he began making attempts to direct the conversation towards religion, his religion. I didn't bite. He questioned, *'You'rrrrre Jewish?'* I was standing their in a black suit, white shirt black hat with my Tzitzit in view. He knew I was Orthodox. The store was in an Orthodox area. This is why he was at this store. He was trolling for Jews to witness to. He wasn't witnessing to people dressed in blue jeans and flannel shirts and tennis shoes.

I replied a bit sarcasticly, *'I'm a mountain man.'*

He responded, *'Oh! You are?'* with a curious look, a puzzled look. He wasn't expecting that response to his question.

I said, *"No! I was only kidding. Why do you think I'm Jewish, already knowing the answer?"*

He responded, *'Because of your long white beard, your black hat, etc.'* He was standing behind me in a check out line with tracks in his hand. He was purchasing nothing. I asked the clerk to page the manager. The manager quickly came to the line I was standing in. I politely registered my complaint. He inquired if the man was purchasing anything. When it was obvious to the manager that the man was not a customer but was just making conversation he showed him to the door.

After I checked out the Christian was waiting for me at the exit from the store into the parking lot. I turned to him eyeball to eyeball and said,

'I understand that you are following your faith. I don't believe in Jesus! I don't want to discuss it! I am in a hurry {hoping he would leave me alone}.'

He got in his truck and drove over to where I was

loading the car and began discussing his beliefs with me again. I did not want to pick a fight with this man. So I invited him to visit JewishPath.org and warned him in the same breath that if he visited he would never be the same again. Visiting was at his own risk!

We each had a few calm parting words...

In the brief conversation with this man, as I continued to load the car, I asked, *'Do you know why Israel is called the Holy Land?'* He did not answer...

Dear Reader, this man is very convinced that he is doing the right thing. Undoubtedly his faith has changed his life which is good, BUT his belief to witness to Jews is VERY, VERY BAD!

I questioned him, *'You're searching for the truth? Right?'*

He stated, {like most Christians do} *'I have already found the truth.'*

I stated, *'You believe you have found the truth. All that you have is based upon belief. In Judaism we know because our faith is based upon historical evidence.'* It is doubtful that the man understood. Holy reader, our deliverance from Mitzriam, our deliverance from the plagues are documented. In addition many non Jews acknowledge a variety of historical proofs as stated in a Christian book written by Dr. Josh McDowel's book, <u>Evidence that Demands a Verdict.</u>

Yet the point to this discussion was the confusing way Christians / Messianics approach what they term the Old Testament. They strongly state it is done away with. Yet they sew their Bible to ours. Why do they do this if it is no longer useful? Why do they teach The Hebrew Scriptures are done away with yet continue to sew their Bible to it? They attempt to witness to Jews with such conviction out of the Book that they believe to be done away with. They attempt to prove that the New Testament is Divinely Inspired by pointing to historical evidences from the Book that they claim to be done away with.

Now, lets get back to the point. Holy reader, **why is the land of Israel called the Holy Land?** Israel is Holy, because The Lord God Separated this parcel of Land from all other lands. We read that The Lord Instructed Avram, '...*Go to The Land that I will show you...*' in Genesis 12.1 We read, '*Avram...set out to go to the Land of Canaan...*' in Genesis 12.5. This is chronologically followed by Genesis Chapter 15. In Genesis 15.7 Avram chronologically was in the land of Eretz Canaan for the first time at the age of seventy. Rabbi Avrohom Davis, The Mesudah Chumash A New Linear Translation Shemot (Hoboken New Jersey, KTVA Publishing House, Inc., 1991) p 142 Also Note: Rabbi Meir Zlotowitz and Rabbi Nosson Scherman, The Artscroll Tanach Series - Bereishis Vol. I(a) (Brooklyn, New York: Mesorah Publications, Ltd. 3rd Impression, 1989), p 514

The Lord God Said in Genesis 15 , '*I Am The Lord Who Brought you out of Ur Kasdim to Give to you this land as an inheritance.*'

Chronologically this occurs before Genesis Chapter 12.6 - 14.24.

Genesis 15.18 - 21
In the same day The Lord Made a covenant from Aleph to Tav with Abram, Saying, To your seed have I Given everything from Aleph to Tav of This Land, from the river of Egypt to the great river, the river Euphrates; Everything from from Aleph to Tav of [the lands of] the Kennith, and Everything from from Aleph to Tav of [the lands of] the Kenazites, and Everything from from Aleph to Tav of [the lands of] the Kadmonites, And Everything from from Aleph to Tav of [the lands of] the Hittites, and Everything from Aleph to Tav of [the lands of] the Perizzites, and Everything from from Aleph to Tav of [the lands of] the Rephaim, And Everything from Aleph to Tav of [the lands of]the Amorites, and Everything from Aleph to Tav of [the lands of] the Canaanites, and Everything from Aleph to Tav of [the lands of] the Girgashites, and Everything from Aleph to Tav of [the lands of] the

Jebusites.

This means that the peace accords in Philistine will not last. It does not matter who signs or agrees to the terms. Why? What does Leviticus 25. 23 Say?

Leviticus 25.23
The land shall not be sold forever; for the land is mine; for you are strangers and sojourners with me.

This means in actuality according to Rashi's interpretation we are merely as foreigners. We are alien residents. In actuality The Land of Yisroel does not belong to anyone but The Lord God!! Rabbi Avrohom Davis, The Mesudah Chumash A New Linear Translation Vayikra (Hoboken New Jersey, KTVA Publishing House, Inc., 1991) p 369 The agreements we make cannot be relied on. We do not have the authority to make these type of agreements. Eretz Yisroel belongs to The Lord God!!

Genesis 13.14,15.

And the Lord said to Abram, after Lot was separated from him, Lift up now your eyes, and **look from the place where you are to the north, and to the south, and to the east, and to the west; For all the land which you see, to you will I Give it, and to your seed forever.**

About 429 years later from Genesis 15 when Avram was 70 years old Moshe climbs Mt Horeb / Sinai to observe the Burning Bush. The deliverance of the People of Israel from slavery in Egypt took place the next year. The People of Yisroel were delivered in 2448 F.C.

Exodus 3.5
And He Said, Do not come any closer; take off your shoes from your feet, for **the place on which you stand is Holy Ground.**

Where was this place? This was Mount Horeb. This is Mt Sinai. This is 'The Place' הַמָּקוֹם Hah Maw Kohm where the ladder extended into the heavens. Yaakov Said, This was the Gateway to Heaven.

While Moshe is their at 'The Place' The Lord God Tells Moshe that He Will bring the People of Israel out of Mitzrim.

Exodus 3.16, 17

Go, and gather the elders of Israel together, and say to them, The Lord God of your fathers, the God of Abraham, of Isaac, and of Jacob, appeared to me, saying, I have surely visited you, and seen that which is done to you in Egypt; **And I have said, I will bring you out of the affliction of Egypt to the land of the Canaanites, and the Hittites, and the Amorites, and the Perizzites, and the Hivites, and the Jebusites, to a land flowing with milk and honey.**

Now, we learn in Parshat Behar Leviticus 25.1 - 26.2) that The Land of Yisroel is required to Have a Sabbath of Rest. What place in the world outside of Yisroel does the Creator of the universe require The People of the land to have a Sabbath of Rest? Does this include ALL the lands Given to The People of Israel by The Lord

God? Perhaps... since the את Eht does not proceed the the Mitzvot here, there maybe room for other possibilities. I am saying that the Mitzvot here could be more absolute. Absolute would be the inclusion of את Eht in Verse one and in verse four. A much greater authority must make that decision.

Leviticus 25.1 - 5

And the Lord Spoke to Moses in Mount Sinai, saying, Speak to the people of Israel, and say to them, When you come into the land which I give you, **then shall the land keep a Sabbath to the Lord.** *Six years you shall sow your field, and six years you shall prune your vineyard, and gather in its fruit; But in* **the Seventh Year shall be a Sabbath of rest to the land, a Sabbath for the Lord;** *you shall not sow your field, nor prune your vineyard. That which grows of its own accord of your harvest you shall not reap, nor gather the grapes of your vine undressed;* **for it is a year of rest to the land.**

The Lord God Establishes Mitzvot regarding the

Land of Israel. The Observances the Lord God Established was ONLY for the Land of Israel. In doing this The Lord God Separated the Land of Israel from all other lands. Rabbi A. Y. Kahan The Taryag Mitzvot (Brooklyn, N.Y. Keser Torah Publications 1987, 1988) pp 201 - 202

Then the year of Jubilee is based on the Seventh year of Rest.

Leviticus 25.8 - 13

And you shall count Seven Sabbaths of years to you, seven times seven years; and the space of the Seven Sabbaths of years shall be to you forty and nine years. Then shall you cause the shofar to sound on the tenth day of the Seventh Month, in the Day of Atonement shall you sound the Shofar throughout all your land. And you shall sanctify the fiftieth year, and proclaim liberty throughout all the land to all the inhabitants of it; it shall be a Jubilee to you; and you shall return every man to his possession, and you shall return every man to his family. A Jubilee shall that fiftieth year be to you; you shall not sow, nor reap that which grows of itself in it, nor gather the grapes in it of your vine undressed. For it is the Jubilee; it shall be Holy to you; you shall eat the produce of it out of the field. In the year of this Jubilee you shall return every man to his possession.

Let's try to understand the possibilities here. The Year of Jubilee is the fifty year that is counted from The Seven Sabbatical Years. **Do you understand how amazing this is? Christians who talk about the Messiah coming in the year of Jubilee would not even have a year of Jubilee if The People of Israel agreed to their doctrines that the Commands, i.e. 'The Law' of The Hebrew Scriptures, i.e what Christians Call 'The Old Testament' were done away with.** They claim Jesus fulfilled all the Law. If this were the case The Observances / Commands that make the Land of Israel Holy / Separated would no longer exist. There would be no Sabbath for the Land every seventh year. Why? This is one of the Laws Christians teach Jesus did away with. There would be no year of Jubilee.

Why? Christians teach the Year of Jubilee is fulfilled. According to them all the Law is done away with. This is why I asked the Messianic if he knew why the Land of Yisroel was the Holy Land. **Christians do you understand that if The Jewish People agreed to stop Observing the Mitzvot of Ha Torah regarding the Land of Yisroel then you would no longer have a Holy Land to visit?** <u>**The Commands that make Yisroel different from all the other places in the world would be gone**</u>. Do you get it? Dear Reader, this is the message we as The People of Yisroel need to be sharing with Christians who try to bushwhack us in shopping stores and airports and who come to our doors to witness about their doctrines. They don't get it!!

Leviticus 27.30
And all the tithe of the land, whether of the seed of the land, or of the fruit of the tree, is the Lord's; it is Holy to the Lord.

The Creator, Takes great offense at the desecration of the laws pertaining to the Land of Yisroel and of the Sabbatical year and our

Sabbaths. In fact, our Beit HaMikdosh is destroyed and most of us are scattered throughout the world because we failed as Jews to properly elevate the Sabbatical year and the Sabbaths.

Holy reader, The Lord took offense at our loathing for His laws. That is why we are so scattered throughout the world! Now believing in Jesus will not reunite Israel or restore the Divine Blessings.

Vayikra 26.42

וְזָכַרְתִּי אֶת־בְּרִיתִי יַעֲקוֹב וְאַף אֶת־בְּרִיתִי יִצְחָק וְאַף אֶת־בְּרִיתִי אַבְרָהָם אֶזְכֹּר וְהָאָרֶץ אֶזְכֹּר:

Mystically we Observe that the Gematria of וְהָאָרֶץ אֶזְכֹּר Vih Haw Aw Retz - Ehz Cor meaning 'And the Land I will remember' is the Gematria of 530. Dear Reader, up until now we may have not given much thought about why the Land of Israel is Holy. However our Creator has NEVER forgotten. He has always remembered the Land of Yisroel. Remembering the Land of Yisroel is very important. This is why saying the morning prayers is very good. In the Morning Prayers we pray for the rebuilding of Jerusalem and for the Land of Yisroel. It is said, An individual who is blind, or one who cannot orient their self, should direct their heart toward our Father in Heaven, as Ha Tenach Instructs, 'They shall pray to the Lord', 1Kings 8.44. One who prayed outside The Land Of Israel should face The Land of Israel, as it is said, And so return to you with all their heart, and with all their soul, in the land of their enemies, who led them away captive, and pray to you facing their land [Israel], which you gave to their fathers, the city which you have chosen, and the house which I have built for your name, 1 Kings 8.48. One who stands in the Land of Israel should face Jerusalem, as it is said, ' If your people go out to battle against their enemy, wherever you shall send them, and shall pray to the Lord toward the city which you have chosen, and toward the house that I have built for your name, 1 Kings 8.44. One who stands in Jerusalem should face the Temple...One who stands in the Holy Temple should face the Holy Place..One who stands in the Holy Place should face the Cover of the Ark...It is therefore found that the entire nation of Israel directs their prayers toward a single location. Baraita

וְהָאָרֶץ אֶזְכֹּר
Vih Haw Aw Rehtz - Ehz Cor
And The Land [of Yisroel] I will Remember
530 = 200ר 20כ 7ז 1א   90ץ 200ר 1א 5ה 6ו

נַסֹּתֶךָ
Nah Sa Teh Chaw / To Try To Test To Prove
530 = 20ך 400ת 60ס 50נ

Mystically our Spiritual test comes everyday. Do we pray? Do we pray for the rebuilding of The Holy Temple? Do we pray for The Holy City? Do we pray for the The Land of Yisroel? In the previous Chapter we donned our tallit and Tefillin. In this chapter we pray with kah vah nah / emotion for The Rebuilding of The Temple, The Holy City and The Holy Land.

When we pray The Lord Remembers. The Lord Forgives. The Lord Blesses!! The Lord Said, אֶזְכֹּר Ehz Cor / 'I will remember'. When The Lord remembers Oo Vah Rayk / He Blesses. The

Gematria for both Ehz Cor and Oo Vah Rayk are 228. Shemot 23.25 reminds us that when we serve The Lord He Blesses us...

Shemot 23.25

וַעֲבַדְתֶּם אֵת יְהוָה אֱלֹהֵיכֶם **וּבֵרַךְ** אֶת־לַחְמְךָ וְאֶת־מֵימֶיךָ וַהֲסִרֹתִי מַחֲלָה מִקִּרְבֶּךָ:

Exodus 23.25

And you shall serve Everything from the Aleph to the Tav of the Lord your God, **and He Shall Bless** *Everything from the Aleph to the Tav of your bread, and Everything from the Aleph to the Tav of your water; and I will take sickness away from the midst of you.*

אֶזְכֹּר

Ehz Cor / *[The Lord Says], I Will Remember!*
228 = 200ר 20כ 7ז 1א

וּבֵרַךְ

Oo Vah Rayk / *and He Shall Bless*
228 = 20ך 200ר 2ב 6ו

When The Lord Said, אֶזְכֹּר וְהָאָרֶץ Vih Haw Aw

Rehzt Ehz Cor / And I will remember the land we see the connection with שָׁב / Shawv meaning Return, Repent, Restore. While the Gematria for וְהָאָרֶץ אֶזְכֹּר Vih Haw Aw Rehzt - Ehz Cor is 530 the Gematria for אֶזְכֹּר Vih Haw Aw Rehzt meaning 'And the land' is only 302. This is the same Gematria relationship with שָׁב / Shawv meaning Return, Repent, Restore.

וְהָאָרֶץ
Vih Haw Aw Rehtz
And The Land [of Yisroel]
302 = 90ץ 200ר 1א 5ה 6ו

שָׁב
Shawv / To repent to return to be restored
302 = 2ב 300ש

The Gematria for both וְהָאָרֶץ Vih Haw Aw Rehzt and שָׁב Shoov are each 302 This directs our attention to the area of wrong doing. What is the area of wrong doing? What would be the wrong thing to do? Forgetting or neglecting or teaching the Mitzvot of Ha Torah, i.e. 'THE LAW' have been replaced. That would definitely be the wrong thing to do! Believing false teaching like this would also definitely be the wrong thing to do! When one does not honor the Sabbatical year and the year of Jubilee by Observing the Commands of The Lord God the sin is against The Lord, against The Torah, The People of Yisroel and AGAINST THE LAND!

Again it is the Torah that directs our lives to repentance, to shuvah. ONLY The Torah, i.e. Law of The Lord can restore the soul, Psalms 19.8

Psalms 19.8
The Torah [i.e. The Law] of The Lord is PERFECT, restoring the soul; the Testimony of The Lord is sure, making wise the simple.

What can we do?
Learning Torah
Observe Mitzvahs
Honor all Jews
Honor Torah Scholars
Encouraging all Jews to:
• learn Torah
• observe mitzvahs

- honor all Jews
- honor Torah scholars
- Unite together
- Uplift The Lord's Holiness

So when we fulfill our areas of responsibilities The Lord will Remember us and He Will Bless us.

When Rabbi Shlomo Carlebach was a young 'timid man' even though that is difficult to imagine. The way he tells stories which just reach out and touch the soul of anyone who listens… it hard to think he was ever timid, Blessed by the Lubavitcher Rebbe and how it changed his life forever. Reb Shlomo was learning in Lakewood. While studying Ha Torah in Lakewood he approached outreach at a distance. He didn't like getting up close and personal with individuals.

Reb Shlomo Said, he had the great privilege of sitting next to the Rebbe and learning with the Rebbe. 'It was Gan Eden'. This means it was like being in Heaven with the Creator. One day while learning together the Rebbe said to him, 'God

Gave you Talent to talk to Yidden. You have to talk to Yidden. 'Right now, the world needs you to talk to Yidden'.

Reb said, *I want you to know the Rebbe gave me a new Neshama.* That day after leaving the Rebbe's presence he felt different. After receiving the new soul he wanted to talk to other Yidden up close. He related suddenly He wanted to tell every Yid he saw there's a great Rebbe. He wanted to stand on his own two feet when talking to individuals up close when he was away from the Rebbe. He said that He would not leave the subway unless he had talked to at least one Yid. He would travel back and forth on the subway searching for a Yid to share with. He would say I'm not leaving until least I talk to Yid.

Back when he was a young man Reb Shlomo said it was the night before Erev Shavuot . At that time Erev Shavuot and Sabbath were Observed together since the were on the same day. After learning he needed to travel home. It was late at night. He wasn't a rich schlepper and didn't have the chutzpah meaning he was not particularly audacious or that he didn't have the guts to borrow money so he took the subway instead of riding in a cab. While taking the subway sitting opposite of him was a young man maybe 20 or 22 years old. He was glowing. He appeared to be Jewish. Rev Shlomo said to him, 'Hey brother I see you're so happy. What's the occasion?

The Young Man Said, *Well, I'm Jewish. I'm so proud to tell you I'm getting married at a [Christian] Church to a non-Jewish girl in the Bronx on the Sabbath. It's a very special weekend for me.*

Reb Shlomo related that he knew it was a very special weekend for him. He said there is only one way of talking to him. Shlomo said, *listen to me. I appreciate it! It is very very special that you're getting married but I feel you should get a blessing from a very holy man before you go to the chupah. Just two stations back is this very holy man. I think our meeting here is providence. Let's go back just two stations and I'll bring you to Rebbe.*

Reb Shlomo said, *I'll never forget it. By that time it was 4:30 am of Erev Shavuot. They went to Rebbe's home. He knocked on the door. The Lubavitcher Rebbe opened the door. How many people have the privilege of Lubavitcher Rebbe, this holy righteous man opening the door for them? Reb Shlomo had his arms around this young man. He spoke to the Rebbe in Yiddish because the young man could not understand.*

The Rebbe asked, *What did you bring me?*

Reb Shlomo said, *The young man needs a little teaching. He's getting married in church on Sabbath.*

The Rebbe said to Reb Shlomo wait outside. He waited until about 7:30 am very close to the door while saying Tehillim. He asked, Do you know what the Rebbe was doing? He was washing out his Neshama / his soul. This was not just a little dust. The Rebbe had to do plastic surgery on his neshama. He had to cut very deep. The Rebbe opens the door. The Young man steps out. The young man's eyes were flooded with tears. The

Rebbe said to Reb Shlomo, Take this young man to the mikvah. The Mikvah was very crowed because that evening was both Shavuot and Sabbath. The 'Rebbe said, Then put Tefilin on with him... The young man returned to Judaism.

Can you imagine what it would be like if you were me and if you were standing in a check out line in a local store in the Jewish Community and Reb Shlomo Carlebach came up and stood in line behind you and began sharing about Judaism? Wouldn't that be wonderful?

Leviticus 27.34
These are the Commandments, which the Lord Commanded Moshe for the people of Israel on Mount Sinai.

Chazak - חזק

GEMATRIA CHART

Letter	Hebrew	Value		Final	
Aleph	א	1			
Bet	ב	2			
Gimmel	ג	3			
Dalet	ד	4			
Hey	ה	5			
Vav	ו	6			
Zayin	ז	7			
Chet	ח	8			
Tet	ט	9			
Yud	י	10			
Chof	כ	20	Final	ך	500
Lamid	ל	30			
Mem	מ	40	Final	ם	600
Nun	נ	50	Final	ן	700
Samech	ס	60			
Ayin	ע	70			
Pey	פ	80	Final	ף	800
Tzzadi	צ	90		ץ	900
Quf	ק	100			
Reish	ר	200			
Shin	ש	300			
Tav	ת	400			

SCRIPTURE INDEX			
Genesis	Page	Genesis	Page
1.2	121	12.5	217
1.4	100	12.6-14.24	218
3.9	65	13.14, 15	219
4.3	74	14.14	91, 95
4.4	28, 75	15	217, 220
4.5	29	15.7	217
4.3-5	26, 28, 40,	15.18-21	218
4.3-5	70, 71, 73	29.11	93
4.7	76	31.23	94
6.9	43	31.24	95
7.2	46	31.32; 37	93
7.2,3	41, 42, 44	31.44	94, 95
8.2	40	31.54	69, 93
8.20	77	32.11	93
9.2-5	26, 49	32.14	38
9.3	40, 45, 46	32.19	38
12.1	217	43.11	38

Genesis	Page	Exodus	Page
43.11	38	39.30	196
46.27	78, 79	40.9	196
49.3	30		

Exodus	Page	Leviticus	Page
3.5	220	1.2	121
3.16, 17	221	1.4	100
12.23	58	3.9	65
19.6	196	4.3	74
20.8	181. 196	4.4	28, 75
23.18	57	4.5	29
23.25	229	4.3-5	26, 28, 40,
26.34	196	4.3-5	70, 71, 73
28.2	196	4.7	76
28.38	196	6.9	43
29.6	196	7.2	46
29.7	196	7.2,3	41, 42, 44
30.12-16	55	8.2	40
30.25	196	8.20	77

Leviticus	Page	Leviticus	Page
9.2-5	26, 49	19.3	161, 179
9.3	40, 45, 46	19.24	196
12.1	217	20.26	193
12.5	217	21.8	194
12.6-14.24	218	22.2	194, 196
13.14, 15	219	22.32	187, 195
13.13	119	22.32	196
13.35,36	120	23.2	196
14.3	142, 143	25.1-5	
14.35-45		25.1- 26.2	221
14.43	133, 144	25.8-13	223
16.3	196	25.10	201, 208
16.33	196	25.23	219
17.10	61	26.42	212
17.11	59, 60	26.43	211
18.30	156	27.30	225
18.30	147	27.34	236
19.2	193		

Deut.	Page	2 Chron.	Page
8.11	158	7.14	194
11.22	158		
11.13-21	203		
15.4-8	33		
31.26	92		
Judges			
3.20	122		
1 Samuel			
2.2	193		
Malachi			
1.11	67		
1.10	67		
Tehillim			
19.8	231		
37.12,24	112		
51	56		
51.17-19	69, 73		
128.2	41		

GEMATRIA'S			
Gematria	Page	Gematria	Page
14	128	498	74
50	121, 128	504	110
50	131, 132	529	138, 139
80	129	530	228
100	180	534	204
104	92, 95	540	157
111	129	541	156, 157
123	140	570	202
123	141, 143	570	207, 208
220	123	570	205, 206
228	229	591	198, 199
302	230	610	129
318	82, 84	675	99
360	123, 132	763	181, 182
397	71	1000	180, 182
419	128, 129	1890	129
493	145, 146		

About The Author

Dr. Akiva Gamliel Belk

Jewish, Husband, Father, Grandfather and Step Great Grandfather.

Graduate:
A.A. Long Beach City College,
B.A. Southern California Bible College,
M.A. Southern California Theological Seminary,
D. Th. Southern California Theological Seminary,
D. Th. Denver Charismatic Theological Seminary

Individual Study:
Rabbi Dovid Nusbaum,
Bais Medrash at Yeshiva Toras Chaim,
Hornosteipler Rebbe, Mordicai Tewerski
Group Study:
Rabbi Yaakov Meyer, Aish Denver
Rabbi Yisroel Engel, Director, Colorado Chabad.

Founder:
Jewishpath.org
Jewishlink.net
7commands.com
Bnti.us

Dean of Jewish Studies

B'nai Noach Torah Institute, LLC – Biblical Online Studies

Author of various books.
bnti.us/books.html

Businessman:
Realtor and Property Investor

Books By Dr. Akiva Gamliel

Gematria And Mysticism IN GENESIS - Book I
This book is the first in a series of five books. Book 1 covers Genesis Chapters 1 through 10. In this series of books the reader will be introduced to truths not discussed among the religions of the world. Hebrew in the Bible unveils answers to many mysteries. The entire Bible is founded upon Genesis, Exodus, Leviticus, Numbers and Deuteronomy and the truths that flow out of these five books is different than the rest of the Bible. Why? There is a system of Hebrew Letters with which each have a numerical value that have the power to reveal interesting and mystifying relationships within the Hebrew Letters, Words, Phrases etc. of the First Five Books. The cost of this book is a small investment for what the reader will learn.

Gematria And Mysticism IN GENESIS - Book II
This book is the second in a series of five books. Book 2 is a continues where Book 1 concluded. Book 2 covers Genesis Chapters 11 through 20. As in the first book the reader will be introduced

to truths not discussed among the religions of the world. Hebrew in the Bible unveils answers to many mysteries. The entire Bible is founded upon Genesis, Exodus, Leviticus, Numbers and Deuteronomy and the truths that flow out of these five books is different than the rest of the Bible. Why? There is a system of Hebrew Letters with which each have a numerical value that have the power to reveal interesting and mystifying relationships within the Hebrew Letters, Words, Phrases etc. of the First Five Books. The cost of this book is a small investment for what the reader will learn.

Mysterious SIGNS Of The Torah in GENESIS

This book is the first in a series of five books. Mysterious SIGNS Of The Torah Revealed In GENESIS is an exploration of Biblical truths organized into the Weekly Parshat study of the Bible. Dr. Akiva Gamliel has been recording and referencing decades of study and research. He has gathered, compiled and organized years of discovery into this mystical book for us to learn, enjoy and share. Many years can pass between one discovery to another which forms a bridge between two discoveries. Revelations are the product of many bridges. Enclosed in this book are some of these special relationships.

Mysterious SIGNS Of The Torah in EXODUS
This is the second in a series of Five Books, God Willing. This book is deep, intense, inspiring and extremely interesting. Yet, it is easy to read and follow. Dr. Akiva Gamliel includes a Gematria Chart in the beginning of the book . Like each of Dr. Akiva Gamliel's Gematria books there are special Gematrias waiting for the Reader to discover. There is a special sweetness in sharing a Torah Gematria / Sign during a wonderful warm Friday evening Shabbat meal or on another occasion.

Mysterious SIGNS Of The Torah in LEVITICUS
This is the third in a series of Five Books, God Willing. This book is deep, intense, inspiring and extremely interesting. Yet, it is easy to read and follow. Dr. Akiva Gamliel includes a Gematria Chart in the beginning of the book . Like each of Dr. Akiva Gamliel's Gematria books there are special Gematrias waiting for the Reader to

discover. There is a special sweetness in sharing a Torah Gematria / Sign during a wonderful warm Friday evening Shabbat meal or on another occasion.

Gematria Azer -
A Taste Of Torah From Genesis

This book is the first in a series of five books. Each Chapter follows the Weekly Parshat with a Torah question, a Gematria or two and a brief discussion. For those that desire each lesson has a matching Video by Dr. Akiva Gamliel Belk, Dean of Jewish Studies at B'nai Noach Torah Institute, LLC.

Gematria Azer -
A Taste Of Torah From Exodus

This book is the second in a series of five books. Each Chapter follows the Weekly Parshat with a Torah question, a Gematria or two and a brief discussion. For those that desire each lesson has a matching Video by Dr. Akiva Gamliel Belk, Dean of Jewish Studies at B'nai Noach Torah Institute, LLC.

Eve Of Creation RESTORED

Good people make bad mistakes. We are at times careless instead of cautious. We hurt those we love. We become angry for no apparent reason and tense without a trigger. We feel frustration! It feels like life has dealt us a loosing hand. We need a new life. We think, what would it be like to have a new life? We day dream of a place and a time that is different than where we are... We feel like we are on an endless downward spiral. It feels like, if there were any hope, it is a great distance away... We are unhappy with our relationship... relationships... our employment... our earning capacity... our children... It's like everything around us smells!

What do we do? How do we face our endless, whatever? How do we put a stop to our seemingly endless downward spiral? The answer is simple. We repair and restore our image of Eve of Creation. Ha Torah Reveals through HOLY Numbers and Letters how to reverse improper behaviors and IMPROVE our selves.

A Sincere Journey Ends Without Jesus

This is an autobiography of my spiritual journey. My journey did not begin with the goal of returning to Judaism. My journey began with a desire to give my Baptist Congregation a historical view of Jesus last six days on earth. My journey has been very challenging for me. If you read this book and if you walk in my footprints believing in Jesus will become a challenge for you also.   The difference is I am on this side of the journey now. I have returned to Judaism. The journey of my life can be of great help to you if you discern there are problems with the story the New Testament story of Jesus.

Would You Like To Be Jewish ?
This book is the first in a series of three books. Many readers would like to know what it is like to be Jewish. Some have tried to learn what it is like to be Jewish.   Some visited with a Rabbi who may have said, something like this, 'Why do you want to convert? Why do you want to be Jewish? We don't do conversions in Judaism.' You ended up walking away disappointed, angered, exasperated, annoyed and very dissatisfied. This book answers questions about what Jewish

believe in a way you will not forget.

Would You Like To Be Jewish 2 ?

This book is the second in a series of three books. This is a continuation of the first book, Would You Like To Be Jewish. In this book we learn that God has always had a plan, even before the beginning of Creation. We learn how God Teaches us to repent when we fail and when we make mistakes. We discover God is very understanding, compassionate and forgiving. We share about fallen angels, , Satan, hell and how to live eternally with God.

PASSOVER –
The LAST SIX DAYS of Jesus Life On Earth

The Gospel Writers each offer a different perspective of Jesus last six days on Earth. They differ some. I offer my own perspective as a Jew that has been on both sides of this discussion. If you are a Christian… If you believe in Jesus this book will be very challenging. I started on this Journey almost 30 years ago with a desire to give my Baptist Congregation a historical view of Jesus last six days on earth. Since then I have returned to Judaism. I share some of the untold stories and fill in some of the blank pages... My journey can be of great help to you if you discern there are problems with the story the story the Christian Writers tell of Jesus last six days on earth.

The Biblical Historical Calendar Book

The Biblical Historical Calendar Book covers many goals for all walks of life. My calender is a religious calendar and a compilation of many prized wild life photographs including trophy Mule Deer, Elk, Rocky Mountain Goats, Coyotes and Foxes and beautiful birds.

The Biblical Historical Calendar Book focuses on the History of the Bible and the beauty of nature. There is a great deal to learn about the Bible's Calendar while at the same time enjoying some breath taking wildlife photographs. This book provide the readers with interesting information about the measurement of time in the Bible and more than a dozen photographs from my prized nature and wildlife photograph collection. Doors open to many special journeys. Walk in the paths of Noah, Abraham and Moses. Learn how today's calendar is much different from the Biblical Calendar. Why the Biblical calendar changed? How that has impacted us.

We will take an adventure with Noah on the ark. We will follow the Children of Israel out of Egypt to Mount Sinai where The Lord Gave us the Commandments. This is a book that every household can and will enjoy for years to come. This is an investment that will pay dividends the rest of your life. The Biblical Historical Calendar Book is a precious tool that offers each of us many dates of spirituality and celebration. I wish you much pleasure and enjoyment as you travel through the history of the Bible.

Order Additional Books At:

http://www.bnti.us/books.html

www.ingramcontent.com/pod-product-compliance
Lightning Source LLC
Chambersburg PA
CBHW071657090426
42738CB00009B/1556